The Perfect System

The
Perfect
System

Syd Kessler

Foreword by
Paul William Roberts

Published in 2000 by Stoddart Publishing Co. Limited
34 Lesmill Road, Toronto, Canada M3B 2T6
180 Varick Street, 9th Floor, New York, New York 10014

Distributed in Canada by:
General Distribution Services Ltd.
325 Humber College Boulevard, Toronto, Canada M9W 7C3
Tel. (416) 213-1919   Fax (416) 213-1917
Email cservice@genpub.com

Distributed in the United States by:
General Distribution Services Inc.
PMB 128, 4500 Witmer Industrial Estates, Niagara Falls, NY 14205-1386
Toll-free Tel. 1-800-805-1083   Toll-free Fax 1-800-481-6207
Email gdsinc@genpub.com

04 03 02 01 00   1 2 3 4 5

Cataloguing in Publication Data

Kessler, Syd
The perfect system
ISBN 0-7737-3235-7

1. Self-realization.   2. Science and psychology.   I. Title.
BF637.S4K47 2000   158.1   C00-930100-3

U.S. Cataloguing in Publication Data
(Library of Congress Standards)

Kessler, Syd.
The perfect system / Syd Kessler. — 1st ed.
[224]p.: ill.; cm.

Summary: A new approach to living for a purposeful life,
from a self-made millionaire.
ISBN 0-7737-3235-7

1. Self-help techniques.   2. Motivation (Psychology)   I. Title.
158 21 2000   CIP

Jacket design: Angel Guerra
Text design and typesetting: Kinetics Design & Illustration
Text illustrations: Crowle Art

THE CANADA COUNCIL | LE CONSEIL DES ARTS
FOR THE ARTS | DU CANADA
SINCE 1957 | DEPUIS 1957

We acknowledge for their financial support of our publishing program the Canada Council, the Ontario Arts Council, and the Government of Canada through the Book Publishing Industry Development Program (BPIDP).

Printed and bound in Canada

To Celia Kessler,
my mother, my friend, my nourishment

Contents

Foreword

by Paul William Roberts

Syd Kessler has been my friend for nearly twenty years. I knew him when he was the undisputed "King of the Jingle," the owner and creative head of an organization that included an advertising and TV/radio production house, along with several recording studios, and he picked up more industry awards annually than could even be displayed. I knew him and worked with him when he forged a partnership with Labatt to create SuperCorp, the largest entertainment and media production company in Canada, with revenues in the hundreds of millions of dollars. I knew him when he left the partnership to embark on ventures at the leading edge of what was then both science and business. And I knew him when he fell sick, forced to watch what he had built from nothing crumbling into dust. I'm happy to say, however, that I still know him as his life takes off on yet another tangent.

Syd has always striven for excellence in whatever he has become involved with: fatherhood, tennis, snooker, conjuring tricks. In life as in business, he doesn't rest until he masters the subject. Thus, no one is more qualified than he to give the advice contained in this book. It is the combined wisdom of someone who has been at the top of his field and also someone who has experienced the depths of personal misery. In my experience, this is unique. Such books are normally written by people whose talents and success lie in the area of writing these books. Syd's talents and enormous success lie in the areas of life skills and business. He knows what he's talking about here, and many of the examples he gives are drawn from his own experiences. Nothing is hypothetical. The Perfect System is not just a theory: it's a set of principles that can be applied in virtually any business or personal situation.

In our own ways, Syd and I have both explored almost every other system there is: Judaism, Sufism, Buddhism, yoga, Taoism, mantra, tantra, yantra . . . But, like the story of the man who spends his life searching for treasure, finally gives up, and then finds it buried beneath his own house, we both found, independently, the tool or key we sought, not in the East, but in the study and practice of Kabbalah, the mystical form of Judaism that underlies all Western esoteric philosophies.

Thus, unsurprisingly, at its core this book is a remarkable synthesis of ancient wisdom and modern physics. Syd calls it the Perfect System, and it is exactly that — a system borne out by life itself, because it is the underlying structure of life itself. For example, I've found the subtle principle of restriction — admirably explained here — especially true and potent, and on many levels. In the situations to which I have applied it, there has frequently been a remarkable outcome, a kind of counter-intuitive tour de force. Indeed, such a jolt of force that I find it hard to believe anyone would not experience as little short of miraculous the sudden enhancement of their efficacy in numerous areas. After grasping and applying what is — and I do not exaggerate — one of humankind's greatest intellectual breakthroughs in understanding the underlying laws of the cosmos, most readers will probably wonder how they ever managed their lives without this knowledge. They will certainly be ever grateful that Syd Kessler took the trouble to share what another man might have jealously guarded for himself or never bothered to analyze in the first place.

Acknowledgements

This book could never have been completed without the assistance, insistence, inspiration, support, and brain power of the following people:

David Kilgour

Paul William Roberts

Kevin Gray

Ron Mandel

Billy Phillips

Michael Ryan

David Morrow

Jacob and Isaac Kessler

Mike Kessler

Ellen Kessler

Marq de Villiers

Nelson Doucet

Ken Wilber

Rabbi Aryeh Kaplan

Rabbi Yehudah Ashlag

Special thanks to:

Rabbi Philip Berg, Karen, Yehuda, and Michael

Rabbi Eugene Weiner and Anita

1

First Thoughts

Fulfillment. We all want it, a sense of completion and contentment. And yet somehow, in the apparent chaos of our busy lives, fulfillment can seem unattainable. Between the demands of work, family, and relationships we find our energies scattered, and often we lose sight of our life goals and settle for quick fixes that ultimately leave us dissatisfied.

It does not have to be this way. For years I had all the optics and apparel of success but still didn't feel fulfilled. I suffered from constant anxiety, frustration, and unhappiness. This is the story of what I did about it. I hope it is relevant to you today. To see how good the fit is, take a moment to look at the statements below. If any of them is true for you at any time in a typical week, then I know you will find value in this book.

- Life and its events appear to be random.
- You don't feel at peace with yourself.
- You don't feel satisfied or complete.

- You feel a little empty inside — unfulfilled.
- A feeling of uncertainty permeates your home, your workplace, or both.
- Even though you may have a loving partner and great kids and good work, you feel that you live in a chaotic, unpredictable world and you are one of its victims.

Anything sound familiar? To most of us, life is often chaotic. We read about it in the newspapers, we see it on the news, we hear about it happening to the people and friends around us, and we experience it ourselves. Someone is killed by a drunk driver. One day business is good, a month later you get laid off. Bad people keep getting richer, seemingly good people keep getting poorer. In my own case, my father dropped dead of a heart attack at forty-nine.

Such events, and the feelings of dread and impermanence that accompany them, permeate our homes and our places of work. Not many of us feel at peace with ourselves. We don't feel satisfied or complete. In fact, if we're honest, most of us have had at times the sensation of feeling empty inside and unfulfilled in life. We live in an unpredictable world and we are its victims — or so it seems.

I was baffled by the continual feeling of emptiness that permeated my own days — and it led me to ask these questions: What is it that I really want out of life? Why is all this mayhem happening to me? What do I do next? This book is for all of you who have asked the same questions and who have not yet found acceptable answers. In short, it is an explanation of how everything works — including us. I know that sounds like a boastful and insane statement but follow my story and me and then decide if I'm right or wrong. After years of study and contemplation, the conclusions I came to were life-changing for me, and I am confident they will be life-changing for you.

~

When I was starting to write this book, I had difficulty deciding whether I should focus on personal experience or on business issues. My learning was relevant to both. This decision, by the way, was purely marketing-driven. I knew that at some point my publisher would want to slot this book into a familiar self-help or business-information category. My problem in focusing on either one of these niches was that, in my opinion, they weren't the story. The story is about my personal experiences and the wisdom I gained from them. I have never seen or created a separation between business and friendship, commerce and relationships. So in spite of the pressure to do otherwise, I stood my ground and did not worry about what niche this book would fit into.

This book is about life. And life, in turn, is about business and friendships and kids and family and pain and happiness, potentiality and completion. I believe that the contents of this book have real power — life-changing power — and this supersedes the notion of marketing niches. I also believe that although, superficially, my experiences may seem very different from yours, we all share the same highs and lows, ups and downs. It's the meaning we bring to them — and take away from them — that counts and eventually creates the real value we are all searching for.

Let me now tell you what this book is not. It is not like one of those books or training courses in which a motivator, a "positive-thinking" guru, teaches his audience a set of skills or techniques that will enable them to better themselves. Usually the instruction is coupled with a series of feel-good motivational exercises that leave people feeling positive about themselves. For a while.

As you have no doubt noticed, there is a whole industry built up around this yearn-and-learn paradigm. There are corporate, life skills, and relationship-training programs in all shapes and sizes. They are offered in all media and are plentiful and easily accessible. You can learn in a classroom, from a CD-ROM, a video, a book, or the Internet. Becoming increasingly popular is asynchronous learning, where you can journey at your own pace in the physical environment of your choice.

However, these programs all fail to provide what I think is the most important aspect of the total learning experience. They speak about the *how* to do and *what* to do but never address the issue of *why* to do. This is the reason why, although many people feel empowered by their new set of specific skills at the end of these courses, in the long term they are left feeling that much hasn't really changed in their lives. For example, a person may have learned how to sell product X more effectively but is still confronted daily by tension and stress in his marriage. The mantra to "think and act positive" doesn't seem to turn a sullen teenager into a model kid overnight. The exhortation to express love all the time isn't potent enough to make a bad working relationship good.

Another problem: the motivational aspect of such training proves in the end to be specious. Talk to graduates of a motivational course a year after they have graduated flying high on motivation. Are they materially and emotionally more successful? In many cases, yes to the former and no to the latter. For the most part they are not satisfied with their lives. They are still unhappy. Their appetite for material acquisition or quick fixes, in spite of everything, is rapacious and they need to keep consuming. They don't "feel" better off than they were before they took the course. The reason is that what we all really want out of life, in fact, has nothing to do with material goods or instant gratification. It is something else. And it is this something else that I will define and try to illuminate in this book.

The Perfect System uses a tool that can, almost miraculously, unlock all the answers to the questions you have been dying to ask all your life yet never found anyone to whom you could pose them. Other systems either do not adequately focus on or, in many cases, do not even *offer* this tool.

There is nothing mysterious about it. It revolves around the simple idea that we all have an inalienable right to ask the question "Why?" — and not to leave the room until we've received an answer that is relevant and makes sense to our lives.

All that is being taught in motivational seminars, continuing education, or corporate training courses is what to do and when and how to do it. But there is a more fundamental question to be asked: Why are we learning this stuff? Why should we treat the information we are learning with any respect? If we were honest with ourselves we would acknowledge that these courses are basically about techniques to manipulate people (buyers, colleagues, bosses, lovers, children) to do what we want them to do (buy more, like us better, give us a promotion, think of us as a team player) all for the sake of our personal achievement. These courses are given names like "Understanding Teamwork," "Becoming a More Motivated Seller," "The Inner Male/Outer Woman," and so on. The problem is that if we don't know the why, then the what and how have no meaning or value to us. Instead of thinking how you can improve your life, try asking yourself some "why" questions.

Why am I at this company working in this job?
Why am I in this marriage or relationship?
Why do I want more responsibility?
Why am I pushing myself so hard?

Why am I here? What is the purpose of my life?
Why am I reading this book?

The answer to the last question, I presume, is that something is missing in your life. And this condition is not acceptable to you — just as it wasn't acceptable to me.

Only when you understand the why of a situation can you begin to have true control and certainty in your life. The why is just a key — but it is the key that will unlock the Perfect System.

And this system is based on nothing less than the totality of physical nature, along with the laws of the universe that govern it. It is based on the way things really work. Like scientists, when we start studying the macro we will invariably begin to understand the micro.

2

Big Bangs and
First Causes

Writing this book is frankly frustrating for me because by its nature it is a monologue, and I am not a big fan of one-way broadcast experiences. I love dialogue, two-way interaction. It is much more satisfying. Because I am a nonlinear thinker, I am not one to accept "what must be," so I have created a mindset that would allow me to feel more comfortable in this one-way milieu. I thus imagine that you are a long-lost friend and we have reunited after many years. I see us sitting at my dining-room table after a great meal. We're no more than three feet apart, and during our supper conversation you have noticed that my eyes are softer, my movements less jerky, and my language more caring. You say, "Something has changed about you. You seem different. What's going on?"

I answer by starting at the beginning . . .

I was born in 1946, in Dundas, Ontario, and grew up a goofy, normal fifties kid in a loving, lower-income Jewish home. I had wonderful parents, and I remember a lot of laughter in our house. My father was a truck driver, and when he died suddenly at the age of forty-nine I was only thirteen years old.

I don't have to emphasize the impact of that one cataclysmic event on an impressionable teenager. My father's death was the seminal, most defining moment of my early life. I became severely depressed and eventually dropped out of school. I spent the next five years working as a labourer — everything from toiling in the pits at a steel mill to being a brakeman for the CNR. At nineteen, however, I got into show business, which in Canada wasn't so much of a business in those days — just as well, too, because I wasn't much of a businessman. There were two reasons for this change of profession. First, I found myself at a family party and met a famous manager of a country star and figured that I knew more than this guy, so in short order I found myself a band to manage. Second, I was getting pretty fed up being a labourer and sensed that it was a dead end and there must be more to be had out of life. So with the combination of youthful hubris and dissatisfaction, and with the aid of some friends, I got my boys — don't laugh, the Gass Company — a recording contract in Los Angeles.

As it turned out, I hadn't spotted the next Beach Boys or the new Doors, but one thing led to another, though not for the band. I was an assistant engineer on a comedy album with a guy who thought he was W.C. Fields (this was L.A., don't forget) and the guys writing the album were also the head writers of a new TV show called *Rowan & Martin Laugh-In*. This guy was so off the wall, as were the recording sessions, that I started throwing out one-liners while running the sound equipment. The writers were impressed with my wit and persuaded me to quit my job in the music business and think about being a comedy writer. I guess you could say they discovered me.

Confidence in hand, knocking on every door of opportunity, I finally landed a job writing radio commercials for what I subsequently found out was America's number-one radio production company. A year later and with a couple of international awards in my pocket, I applied with twenty others for a job to develop a TV game show for ABC. I got the job, which lasted about six months, but all the while I kept my hand in radio by doing commercials freelance. It took me a while, but by the early seventies, I understood the business well enough to start my own production company in Toronto. By the eighties, I owned and ran the top radio and music production company for advertising in Canada.

At thirty years of age I was already a millionaire. By the time thirty-five rolled around, I was doing about $10 million yearly in sales. It was during this heady period, the late eighties, that I was approached by executives of the Labatt Brewing Company in Toronto who were looking to set up an entertainment division. They wanted me to run this new enterprise. I was flattered, but I refused their offer because I had always been an entrepreneur and couldn't see myself as anyone's employee. However, I did counter their proposal with one of my own: a partnership. Much to my surprise, they agreed. This was highly unusual for such a massive corporation.

With the support and vision of Labatt president Sid Oland, I was able to grow a new company — aptly named SuperCorp — on the back of my existing business. Sid was a brilliant corporate leader and, to my good fortune, shared my vision for this new venture. I swiftly reached the giddy heights of $150 million yearly in sales, mainly through acquisitions. My strategy was to buy top-notch companies in the advertising production business. Simple enough, but if others had thought of it they hadn't done it. At the company's zenith we controlled 68 percent of all broadcast advertising produced in Canada and even an unheard-of 2 percent in the United States. Not only did we own what was generally perceived to be the best radio and TV production companies in Canada and the States but we also owned a world-class animation house and Canada's largest independent media–buying house. By the fourth year of our relationship, $500 million was revolving in the business accounts annually.

This period saw the peak of my personal power. I was wealthy and influential, had a great wife, two amazing kids, a beautiful home, and all the other trappings and distractions that money could buy. But — and clichés become clichés because they're true — inside I felt empty. It was a classic case: here I was with everything I had worked so hard to attain, yet I had never felt less fulfilled. These feelings continued for six years, during which time I sold my shares in the Labatt partnership.

There were two reasons for my doing this. First, a person who did not share my vision had replaced Sid Oland; and second, I saw the world of broadcast advertising losing its historical power to the new narrowcasting opportunities (one-to-one marketing, the Internet, e-commerce, etc.) then being enabled by a new digital technology. With the share money from SuperCorp, I bought into a small multimedia company that, under the leadership of myself and my long-time partner Salim Sachedina, had first-year contracts potentially worth more than $300 million with American companies such as U.S. West, Wal-Mart, and Dow Jones. The future, yet again, looked bright.

I felt invincible. I was Superman: I smoked four packs of cig-arettes a day, worked seventy-hour weeks, and never got sick. It seemed as if there was nothing I couldn't accomplish. My body, however — which I'd always been oblivious to — had a dif-ferent view. It was 1994. I was now in my late forties, so this kind of business growth, and the G-force pressures that go with such supersonic acceleration, were starting to affect me physically, even though I ignored the signs at first. Soon, though, I couldn't ignore them. Even this is an understatement: suddenly, I felt as if I'd been hoisted up onto the business end of a Kryptonite suppository.

I wasn't just sick. I was really sick. For a start, the doctors informed me, I'd become diabetic. Then, while trying to get my diabetes under control, they discovered that I had a rapidly deteriorating nerve condition called stenosis of the spine. This is a disease in which some of the nerves in the spine are squashed by an abnormal buildup of calcium deposits. When a nerve is damaged and can't communicate with the muscle, atrophy sets in. It is rare, but this doesn't recommend it. There are better diseases. Even its discovery was a fluke, because I experienced no pain. I knew that I was starting to limp, but as usual I was so focused on the outside world that I denied it. I buried it. Yet the doctors discovered that I had lost 60 percent of the use of the muscles in my right leg and 40 percent in the left. They recommended immediate corrective back surgery — a major, and tricky, operation — to prevent any further deterioration and the loss of the use of the rest of the muscles in my legs. Basically, this involved scraping away surplus calcium suffocating the nerves in my spine.

I was home convalescing for about a year. It was the first time since leaving school that I hadn't worked. I wasn't used to it. I plunged into a horrible depression, which, we subsequently discovered, was caused by the diabetes. But the thing about depression is that you don't care what's causing it: you're too depressed. And not only was I depressed, I was also increasingly frustrated, as I sat — or lay — on the sidelines, watching the awful spectacle of my new business slowly sinking below the horizon. There was nothing I could do about it, either. I couldn't move. I felt completely impotent.

It was also the first time that I'd had to contemplate, rather than perform, my own role in a business, and it was frightening. I was the force majeur, it seemed, and without me the enterprise simply lost momentum, grinding slowly to a halt. All that I had built over twenty-five years, all that was solid, melted into air before my eyes until it was merely a blur. There was nothing left. My family was intact and supportive, but frankly "I was what I built." And what I built was crumbling and, along with it, my self-esteem.

Oddly, however, the next thing I remember is that I slowly started to feel better emotionally. Medication had begun to control my depression, and I noticed my stamina return, albeit gradually. Piece by piece, I started to put my professional life back together, though not without the help of friends. Soon, as it does, one thing led to another, and I was approached by a wonderful, brilliant guy, Michael Ryan at KPMG (the world's largest professional services company) to assist in building a Canadian digital strategies practice he had just started. This practice conceived and developed models of commerce made available by the advent of cybertechnology — namely e-commerce — and brought them to organizations that needed advice on how to deal with the impact of such forces on their world.

This man knew my whole history, both medical and business, yet he didn't care that I couldn't work full days. He simply wanted my experience and vision. A new horizon was exactly what I needed at that point, so I agreed to join him. I have been there for more than two years now, and the practice has grown to be extremely successful. Professionally, I managed to transfer my past skill sets into the new digital arena. Physically, I still have good and bad days, but I can live with that. I am truly grateful for all that I have.

What I'm going to tell you now may sound odd, but it is important. Over the course of the whole nightmare roller-coaster ride of the past four years, since I became sick and watched my business collapse, I have come to feel more empowered than ever, both personally and professionally. I have never felt more in control of my destiny. Those years were like the time at university that I missed out on, giving me the opportunity to step back and observe, reflect, and clarify. I saw business and my professional life with a new perspective. But that was not all I had the time to learn. As you'll see, there was another catastrophic event during this period, and it forced me to probe a lot deeper inside myself, below the surface of my aptitude at business. This event was a crash course in self-realization that took me to the very limits of human understanding and beyond.

The craziest thing of all about those years of disaster, however, is that none of my learning came from the events I have just described to you. I had tumultuous ups and downs, to be sure, a really stomach-churning ride. But, when all is said and done, what can you really learn from a roller-coaster ride? It goes up, it goes down, and it goes around. That's it. It taught me nothing — nothing at all. And the reason for this is that I was blind to the reality that lies beneath the surface of life. I was hip to the carnival of change that goes on up here above, but I couldn't see the more constant truth that exists below, the truth that in fact controls all the rest. I thought I knew the rules of the game, but the truth is that few of us do. We don't even know the real game. My new empowerment thus came from a new understanding of the world that started to dawn on me when one day, a little over three years ago, I found myself crying uncontrollably at the wheel of my car.

~

It was just after my mother passed away. She died in 1997 at the age of eighty-three, so it was hardly a premature or unexpected death. I was fifty. But we were very close and had gone through a lot together over the years since my father passed away. She was tragically young to be a widow, and ill equipped to become a single parent. Yet I thought I knew and understood my relationship with her. I'd certainly had the time. She lived a relatively healthy life, but near the end she slowly succumbed to congenital heart disease. I imagined I was prepared for her death, but I wasn't. It affected me deeply, in a place I'd never visited before.

And so, six months after her passing, I found myself driving home and crying just thinking about her. I couldn't stop the tears. You know the kind: you're not so much crying as being cried. It was like trying to hold back the ocean tides. Suddenly, I missed her so much, so very much. I hadn't expected this at all. Her dying affected me in a most unimaginable way. I wasn't prepared for it. There was a raw, aching void inside me. I'd survived illness, depression, the loss of twenty-five years' work and my business, I'd taken them all in stride, but now all of a sudden I was feeling devastated by her passing.

Eventually, one of my friends noticed how awful I looked. Frankly, I told him, I was scared because of this weird over-reaction, this intense grief that I suddenly found myself suffering. His response was nothing like what you'd expect. It took my breath away. It was so sage, so true, that I can honestly say it literally changed my life, forcing my mind through a dramatic 180-degree shift in all that I thought I knew. It was one of those moments you know full well that you'll never forget.

My friend just looked at me and said, "Of course you're devastated, you putz. You haven't just lost your mother, you've also lost your physical creator." He was absolutely right. I was attached to my mother in a way that was more than just the usual mother-son relationship. Where other relationships are more like two planets in the same orbit, we were like the earth and the moon. I had an affinity with her, a bond that superseded her physical presence and even all the experiences we'd been through together. With some relationships, the other person is part of you, and you are part of them. You're often only aware of it when they're gone. Then, all of a sudden, the whole universe seems out of joint. Everything is somehow wrong. I'm sure you've felt this. It's pretty much the same as the feeling you get when you first meet someone and yet suspect that you've known them forever. It happens with places, too: you go somewhere new, yet you instinctively know where everything is, what it's about. The place is more inside you than it is outside, and the sensation triggers a cognitive mechanism beyond your five senses. You and the place or the person are instantly one. You are identified with each other. That's how it was with Mom and me — a transcendent identification that defied explanation.

Just as profound was my sense that at this time and place in history, as a society, we were in an absolute state of denial regarding this idea that we are inextricably joined to everything that came before us, all that we emerged from. The brilliant philosopher and author Ken Wilber succinctly described the concept when he wrote the following in his book *The Marriage of Sense and Soul*:

> Each element [in the physical world] is a whole that is simultaneously a part of another whole: a whole atom is part of a whole molecule, a whole molecule is part of a whole cell,

a whole cell is part of a whole organism, and so forth. Each element is neither a whole nor a part, but a whole/part. This establishes an irreversible hierarchy of increasing wholeness, increasing holism, increasing unity and integration. Each time we grow we differentiate ourselves from the where and what we came from. Not disassociate, for disassociation creates a disconnect from true reality.

It made sense on a theoretical level, but on a more mundane and practical level, how far was I willing to go back before starting to dissociate from where I had come? If I was connected to my mother, then surely I had a connection with her mother, and with her mother's mother, and so on and so forth. How far was I willing to follow the line of affinity?

Such new questions and understanding began me on the journey of self-knowledge that led eventually to the ideas that inform this book. This journey overhauled my very being, changed everything, made me new. It challenged me intellectually, emotionally, and spiritually. It changed my relationship with my family and my feelings about my work. In the end, it changed my expectations of life. It was, as they say, just what the doctor ordered — not that any doctor ordered it. I started to think seriously about and to question those things that existed at the very core of my being and were what I not only believed but believed in. In short (the French always have a term for this kind of thing), my raison d'être, my purpose in existing, suddenly became a pressing issue. But most important, I realized that there was a me separate from the physical me. I was more than just my body. I had sensed this truth for a long time, of course, but I'd never experienced the reality of it.

~

Don't get me wrong, though: I hadn't been a robotic sociopath since my father's death. When I was sixteen, I paid good, hard-earned money to see a psychiatrist. The sessions lasted six whole months, but I never felt I was getting value for the money. He kept telling me I was a square peg trying to fit into a round hole, and "therapy" consisted of trying to mould me into a round peg. Even though I was just another confused, insecure sixteen-year-old, naive as a baby, I knew instinctively that the psychiatrist was dead wrong. I knew that in order to solve "my problem," I had to find a square hole, not become a round peg.

In retrospect, however, I am forced to admit that my sessions with this out-to-lunch shrink were my first foray into what was to be a lifelong quest for the meaning of life. By the time I was in my thirties, I knew enough to understand that the most important motivation driving me — and I did feel driven — was a need to transform the cataclysm of my father's death into something of value, to give it a meaning in my life. I'd created a twisted, largely unconscious paradigm for myself in which it was Dad's death that had enabled me to fulfill my destiny of becoming rich and famous. My father died so that I could be successful. The Freudians have a term for this, I believe — some kind of martyr syndrome. Whatever it was, this paradigm became my way of making sense out of that which otherwise seemed senseless — and thus allowed me to make sense of my life.

We all create these little systems of meaning in one way or another. But a paradigm is really just a box, and a box is limiting by its very nature. It's a four-sided container. It's a rationalization, for how else can we make sense of something inherently nonsensical? Ultimately, then, our paradigm is just our little personal trick for emotional survival. It may get us through the night — often for years — but it isn't really true. It's not real.

But there were many stations other than just this little panacea along the road I'd been on. When your hobby is trying to make sense of life, you tend to try anything, and I've tried most of what's been available in my time. I've covered a lot of ground — or had it dug out from under me.

I was raised a Conservative Jew, but I left the fold in my teens. During my twenties, I must have investigated virtually all forms of religion and belief, in a kind of conspicuous spiritual consumption. In reality, I was a spiritual materialist: what I was investigating was still out there; it didn't really affect me in here. I suppose that I didn't actually find any genuine kind of intellectual, philosophical connection until I was in my thirties, when I discovered Sufism. Sufism was originally a tenth-century mystical offshoot of Islam. It is not easily defined, for it is not a religion, nor does it have a doctrine per se. Sufism is a way of looking at the world and a way of living in the world. I was attracted to it because it fit intellectually. Not completely, but it was a good start.

Then, when I was in my early forties, I finally found a spiritual and intellectual haven, a nexus of ideas and emotions I could live with, in the mystical form of Judaism known as Kabbalah. I felt at home with it, though not because it resembled the religion I had grown up with. It did not. Let me give you an example of why I felt so comfortable with it. *The Zohar*, the main scriptural text of Kabbalah, states that we all have our own personal "frequency" relating to God. The idea is a bit like the concept of radio waves: we each vibrate and resonate at a different frequency, and that is why there are so many different spiritual paths. None of them is exclusive, just different. For me, because I had delved into so many other forms of spirituality, each valid in its own way, this viewpoint had resonance. It explained why other great paths had not led me anywhere, and why this ancient wisdom of the Jews was intellectually and emotionally spot-on.

So I threw myself wholeheartedly into Kabbalah, studying and learning much that was new to me. I hope eventually, if you have not already done so, you will choose your own, different path: perhaps even a nonspiritual one. The fact that I have landed in a Kabbalistic space is relevant only as a historical reference point. It gave me a different frame of reference and added to my arsenal of life experiences. In any case the subject of spirituality is a hot button and not one I wish to push. I do not intend this book to be spiritually or religiously biased. It is fact-biased. My search has always been for objective truth, not subjective opinion. That means that I am committed to the idea that truth for me has no real value unless it is also truth for you.

I had all this information, yet it took my mother's death to suddenly make sense of it and to embody it in my life. Before this wrenching moment, I had absorbed a lot of knowledge, to be sure, but I had not yet converted it into wisdom. In other words, I was smart, but I wasn't wise. This state, for me, was exemplified by an inability to see the big picture. It wasn't a universal truth I was dealing with, only a gospel according to me, only a truth that made sense of my particular life. There was always a sneaking suspicion that this wasn't enough, that I was basically lying to myself — and, furthermore, that this dishonesty was not just keeping a good man down, it was also keeping him away from true happiness. In a nutshell, I was somehow blinded by the obvious.

But what was it before my mother's death that had prevented me from connecting with this truth?

For a start, I began to see that I invariably found myself caught up in a kind of "rationalization loop." For as long as I could remember, whenever I was unhappy I had always tried to look for a new point of view or a different frame of reference to help me out of that state. I searched for this different mental landscape, and when I found it I genuinely believed that I was looking out of a window, while in fact I was only looking into a mirror. Presented there was merely what I thought I wanted to see. But it was comforting and comfortable, so those illusory images became my personal and self-perpetuating form of truth. In many ways, I was a prisoner in the most dangerous jail of all, because it appeared to have no bars and I wasn't aware of not being free. I believe that most of us live in this state of reality denial.

Yet, as I've said, the secret to my eventual escape and its concomitant freedom lay in the blaze of truth that surrounded my friend's sage observation: not only had I lost my mother, I had also been separated from my physical creator.

~

This was just the beginning, though, because from that moment on, many, many things started to make sense to me for the first time. My first revelation was that we must all necessarily have, in some extraordinary way or other, a far more profound affinity with and connection to our physical creator — whether or not we're aware of it. This underlying truth is one of the prime reasons our relationship with our mothers is so complex. It is why orphans historically have such an intense desire to locate their birth mothers. Extending this thought, it occurred to me that there was a logical argument to be made for the fact that we actually have not one but two physical creators: the birth mother and the original, universal Creator, the One who created all material existence, including our birth mothers.

This primal Creator is tough to conceive of, however, because he, she, or it existed before the Creation itself, before time, space, and consciousness. I am not talking about a religious construct here. This Creator could, indeed, be the cause of the very first event in the universe, the event that physicists call the Big Bang, or multiple Big Bangs, according to something called the inflation theory. From this event came, ultimately, not just our foremothers and forefathers, not just you and me, but also the world we live in and the very universe (or "multiverses") in which we exist.

It's a Big Thought, but not too big a thought for the human mind to grasp. That's why I initially looked to the field of science for an answer — or at least the beginning of one. I needed an answer that was not airy-fairy but comprehensible. Not something I could believe in but something I could know with certainty. A linear understanding that didn't require me to make a leap of faith. Leaps of faith are sometimes necessary but they require us to pass over the abyss of reason to get to the other side. It was in reason that I needed to land. I acknowledge that science is predictive and theoretical, that it is a rationalization and not always real proof. But this predictability has allowed us to build bridges, light bulbs and computers. The laws of physics are perfect in the sense that they consist of general rules that have been consistent from the beginning of Creation, rules that are never broken, a connectivity that is flawless and a causality that is certain. I knew both instinctively and intellectually that I had to use science as my starting point.

The next question for me to answer was: What exactly do I or can I know about the First Creator? Since I am by personality a linear, logical thinker, it was natural for me to turn first to science for help. However, right from the beginning I ran into problems. Science did not like the terminology I was using.

Science and the concept of a Creator did not compute. Science was prepared to tell me what happened 0.003 seconds after the Big Bang. It could even speculate on how the Big Bang happened, but it refused to discuss what or who caused this Big Bang, or why. That wasn't the business of science! So I was forced to change my terminology. Instead of trying to find out about the First Creator, I plugged in the words *First Cause*. I soon found that extracting information got somewhat easier.

I first learned that this First Creator/First Cause had everything and indeed was everything. Physics verifies this concept by stating that in the beginning there was no lack: all space, time, energy, and matter were within what is called one singularity — this energy was compressed into something smaller than one-trillionth the size of the head of a pin. I also learned that this First Creator/First Cause was the First Cause of all subsequent effects.

This point, the beginning of physicality and of time, space, matter, and consciousness, would become my flashpoint of investigation and learning. Anything before it was unfortunately hypothetical, ephemeral, and too abstract to build a rational case on. So I planted my intellectual flag and prepared to move on to further discovery.

I then found out that, in this great act of creation, the First

Creator/First Cause manifested itself as an explosion, not an implosion. It was a burst of "out-giving" that kept on giving and apparently kept nothing back for itself. It makes sense because true creation seeks no return.

I also knew that, somehow, I had a relationship with this First Creator/First Cause. I further sensed that this relationship was not only non-physical, quantum, and intuitive but also, in strange contrast, had the dynamic of a genuine physical memory carried in my DNA. It was the same kind of deep intuitive/molecular remembrance that I had felt in connection with my mother: in some arcane way, part of the First Creator/First Cause's essence was simultaneously part of me, both physically and nonphysically. This revelation of both being and belonging infused me with a joy of truth that I had never felt before.

Modern physics seemed to validate this idea, too — though inadvertently — with the empirically provable proposition that the whole universe and everything in it, regardless of distance or dissimilarity, is integrally connected and emanates from a single source. This may sound like mysticism, but it's actually hard science, the so-called new physics, and derives from the following postulation made in the 1960s by Irish physicist John Stewart Bell: "Every particle in the Universe is able to communicate with every other particle regardless of time and space." It's known as Bell's theorem, and it has been proven true for atomic and subatomic particles. I am not trying to show off my scientific knowledge — it's just that I had to learn some of this material to validate my proposition — but do take away with you the important aspect of Bell's theorem, at least as far as we're concerned here: that at a deep and fundamental level the separate elements and parts of the universe are connected in an intimate and immediate way.

I also found this interesting statement by the British scientist

Sir Martin Reese: "The atoms in the remotest quasar or in the early 'Big Bang' are governed by the same laws as atoms we can study in the laboratory."

There were as well many very similar pieces of evidence to indicate a pervasive connectivity in the universe, and soon I became intellectually confident about my initial speculations. I also became more comfortable with the idea that if I had some sort of affinity with the First Creator/First Cause — and I knew I did — then it followed that I would also have an affinity with its system, because I would also be in and of that system.

I felt I had the first piece of a puzzle in place. I was exhilarated, but I was driven to find out more about this First Creator/First Cause.

Affinity with the First Cause/First Creator

3

The Perfect System?

Whose or what's will was behind the mighty event of Genesis has always been a mystery — indeed, the ultimate mystery. And what also is still in doubt, as it always has been, is whether there is a reason behind the Creation, and whether any kind of consciousness was involved in the act. Here, humankind is divided by three opinions. One holds that we and our world are a byproduct of a random, serendipitous event. The second holds that this event was purposeful and that a supernal will was behind the Creation. The third holds that either of these could be true. "I don't know" is, I'm inclined to add, perhaps as valid as the first two. These opinions presented me with a major barrier on my path to objective truth. I call this obstacle the Great Bugaboo: What or who is this thing called God, and what place does he/she/it have in the creation story?

It is a key question and definitely deserves an answer. The answer, however, is that I unfortunately have no objective answer. This word *God* triggers such uniquely individual imagery and such a profoundly emotional response that it is impossible to come up with any single definition that will satisfy a large audience. Whether God exists or is just a psychological projection or philosophical abstraction is not the issue. So I need you to put aside the word and concept of God for the sake of our inquiry. Our purpose here is not affected by whether a thing called God exists or interacts in our lives, whether it is in a human or supernal form, or whether it created the physical world. It is simply not essential to the ideas currently being presented.

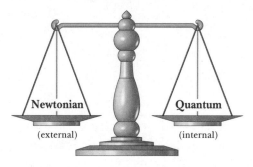

Our only concern is that, after the Creation, a system existed, a set of physical rules that kept the whole machine working. Remember: this system is perfect in the sense that it consists of general rules that have been consistent since the beginning of Creation, rules that are never broken, a contiguity that is flawless, and a causality that is almost certain. And with the contemporary discovery of the principles of quantum mechanics (a branch of physics that focuses on the indeterminate nature of physicality), we learn that both systems are part and parcel of this one universal Perfect System. As we go deeper into this understanding you will start to comprehend the profound, and seemingly impossible, partnership between Newtonian and quantum physics, the relationship that combines supposedly mutually exclusive opposites — order and entropy, predestination and free will. We will see how they coexist, producing a state of predictability and creativity at the same time, and how these perfect relationships and laws of the universe are as pertinent to humans as they are to molecules and atoms. They will become our key, our guide, and our road map to personal fulfillment, certainty, and control.

Let me now reiterate what we have learned so far:

*Something was created out of nothing
(from non-physicality to physicality).*

⇩

The First Cause had and was everything — a totality.

⇩

*Then there was an explosion — a movement outwards,
not inwards.*

⇩

The First Cause kept nothing back for itself.

⇩

*According to our observations, Creation was the beginning of
time, space, and matter and therefore became the First Cause
of all future causes and effects.*

⇩

*With the act of Creation came the irreducible laws and rules of
the physical universe — a Perfect System was manifested.*

⇩

*Everything falls under the governance of the omnipresent and
absolute laws of the Perfect System.*

⇩

*This Perfect System came before the concepts of religion and
spirituality. Which leads to one final point:*

⇩

*The Perfect System is not human-made, it is merely
human-observed and human-chronicled.*

As my understanding of these matters grew, I came to regard the world, the universe, and all that lived within its order of physical laws as part of this Perfect System — a system, furthermore, that could be both observed and learned from.

By observing the "way things work and have always worked," I gradually realized that I could correlate and use the knowledge gained from my observations to answer my most profound questions. Big questions like, "Why am I here? Why is there pain in my life? Where am I going — and where did I come from?" I saw that if all of us could learn to keep focused on the big picture and to harness its information, earned from the study of its structures and interacting systems, then we would have the ability to convert our viewpoint of the world from one of apparent chaos and uncertainty to a new, more dynamic, fundamental truth. This is a world of laws and rules, a world that allows for the coexistence of opposites to interact in a creatively tense harmony. A world of absolute stability and uncontested chaos. A world of machines and Shakespeare. A world of light and darkness. If we could use this wonderful (literally full of wonder) understanding we could, by some measure, control chaos and uncertainty. We would become modern-day alchemists, converting the base metals of potential into the gold of actualization. Dreams would no longer be for dreaming: anyone and everyone would have the ability to make them come true.

In simple terms, for me, it meant that I didn't have to be afraid anymore. There was hope, because I saw that this Perfect System had within it all that was necessary to become the ultimate instruction manual for life. It seemed so obvious, waiting there to be found. The laws and rules of the physical world were not just for the physical universe surrounding us but also for us, because we are all a part of the same physical universe. We are all made of the same physical components. The same atoms and molecules that can be found in a rock are also in the human body. It was just as Sir Martin Reese had said: the rock and the human are affected by the same physical rules and laws that govern the universe. We come in different shapes, sizes, and conditions, and at different levels of animation, but we are all equal participants within the omnipresent laws of our universe.

Just as exciting was to find that, once one has understood the principles of the Perfect System, problems and adversity become simply convertible opportunities for ultimate success. This has always been believed in the Orient, where the ancient Chinese ideogram for *crisis* indicates that it equals *opportunity*.

~

Perhaps an analogy will best describe the kind of change in focus and ability that you can acquire after grasping the laws of this Perfect System. If you have ever driven a rental car in France, you will know that it is next to impossible to find your way through a small French town (think of all the chase scenes you have seen in the Inspector Clouseau movies). The streets are circular and twisting. Maps do you little good. You are simply at the mercy of circumstance — and French driving. But imagine, before entering the town, being able to elevate yourself over the city and get the big picture of the town's street layout. You would be able then to descend and to execute the most expedient, least irksome, and quickest route through the town.

Using the Perfect System, this same big-picture skill can be easily employed for quick and successful manoeuvring through both business and personal turmoil. No matter what the situation — whether you are confronted with a difficult co-worker, financial problems, misbehaving children — you will be able to rise above the moment and see the most efficient path to a successful conclusion.

This is just one of the extraordinary abilities that anyone can acquire once they understand this system. Perhaps the best news about the system is that its rules and laws are foolproof. We're using them already in a sense, because the harmony of this universe we live in operates by them and by nothing else. This is what I found so elegant about it all, so perfect: it *must* work because it has always worked. These rules and laws have not changed since the beginning of time. In this fact lies the ultimate validation of the system, its undeniable truth — and the power of that truth.

~

If I am sounding a little too passionate, forgive me, but this information is so spectacularly life-changing that just writing about it, my enthusiasm wells up uncontrollably. And I don't mean to be preachy, either: I am not trying to convince you of anything because, truly, I have nothing to gain by doing so now. You've got the book in your hands: you or somebody else has already paid for it. All I ask is that you consider its content. The system works. Use it, try it, and see for yourself. Of course, if the system you are already using in your own life is working for you — if it is bringing you the maximum of certainty, success, and fulfillment — then, frankly, you don't need this information. But if my journey of discovery has resonated with you intuitively or intellectually so far, then read on. I promise you the fun has just begun!

4

Cause and Effect

Because the First Cause was literally the First Cause, it had no inherent relationship with the concept of being an effect. It was not part of its experience or energy consciousness. As the old joke goes, it didn't have ulcers, it gave ulcers. I have already discussed our affinity with the First Creator/First Cause. It is this affinity that makes us hate being treated as mere objects that are acted upon or that just react to the actions of others. We don't like it when things are done to us. It makes us feel alienated. This induces systemic uncertainty and a sense of being out of control because when we are effects we are disconnected from our affinity with the First Cause.

Imagine this: you have just had a really hard day at the office and you walk through your front door to a house full of screaming, hyperactive kids all demanding your attention. They don't care about what you've done all day or how you are feeling — they care only about what they're doing right now and how they're feeling. What to do? Shriek at them to leave you alone and barricade yourself in your room? Give in to their demands? Distract them somehow?

There are countless examples of this kind of event. We have all been in a situation in the workplace where our bosses or co-workers irrationally put the blame on us for an event that was totally out of our control. I know now that this effect principle was the reason I did so poorly in high school. In those days (the early sixties) education was a classic "broadcast" experience. The teacher spoke, and we did. There was almost no interaction, no dialogue. I felt totally out of control of my experience at school.

Later on, when I was in my twenties, this theme followed me into a love relationship. She was a beautiful young woman and it was my first experience living together. It didn't last long. The beginning of the end was on the day (and I can hear her words in my head as I retell the story) she started to accuse me of being insensitive to her needs. She was harping at me about not being loving enough, not sharing enough. It made me angry and frustrated because I felt that I never had a chance, because frankly I didn't know what she was talking about. All she had to do was tell me what this thing called sensitivity was and I would have tried to express it. Somehow she confused me with Kreskin the mentalist and thought I should know telepathically what to do. I felt powerless. Indeed, I felt like an effect, and it was a very painful experience.

Just consider moments in your past or everyday life when you have been an effect and not a cause. Take a moment and, in a notebook, write a list of such situations from the last week or month. Most of the items on your list will no doubt reflect those discomfiting moments in situations both private and professional when you should have been firmly at the helm but felt instead frighteningly out of control — if not distinctly put upon, used, or even abused.

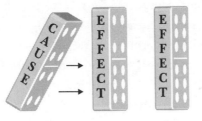

Let me explain, using the time-honoured illustration of dominoes and their famous effect. When the first cause domino falls on us (the "effect" domino) it is painful and makes us feel out of control, put upon, abused. What often exacerbates the pain of these situations is that we are not expecting the sheer force of the impact. We don't like the sudden realization that we're mere pawns in someone else's game, either. We don't like it because, fundamentally, part of us is like the First Cause. I am reiterating this point because understanding it is key to our strategy for success.

A vital piece of the puzzle is now in place. Please make sure that you thoroughly grasp the meaning and importance of this truth before proceeding: We are all a part of the First Cause and the First Cause is a part of us.

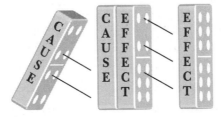

Using the same illustration, I now want to point out a hidden truth embodied in the middle domino. This middle domino has the innate potential to be both an effect and a cause. That's the secret: every action we take has the potential to be either a cause or an effect. We simply have to be aware at all times that we have a choice. We have free will and we can exercise it by remembering that our deep and intrinsic affinity with the First Creator/First Cause gives all of us the potential to create (to exercise that free will). We know that free will exists because it is part of the Perfect System. It is an essential element of quantum mechanics and de facto must be an endemic element of the First Cause. Free will is one of the incontestable partners in the seemingly impossible alliance of causality and indeterminacy — Newtonian and quantum physics.

It would be appropriate at this time to define those two terms for you. In simple and general terms, as I understand it, Newtonian physics describes how objects react when acted upon. It is the picture of the clockwork mechanism of the universe, the explanation of everyday phenomena. These principles relate to objects that are as small as an atom and as large as planets. Newtonian physics describes notions such as energy, motion, work, gravity, and cause and effect. Newtonian physics leads to the idea that, in the physical world, every action and reaction are predictable. This idea is called determinism, the view that every event or act is the inevitable consequence of antecedents.

Let's now take a look at what is termed the new science. Quantum mechanics, relativity, and superstring theory are de rigueur in this contemporary thinking. Quantum mechanics deals with the movement of subatomic particles. Basically, as explained in Michio Kaku's book *Hyperspace*, "we can never know simultaneously the velocity and position of a subatomic particle." This is the Heisenberg uncertainty principle. The uncertainty principle means that we can never be sure where an electron is or what its velocity is. The best we can do is to calculate the probability that the electron will appear "at a certain place with a certain velocity." Therefore, quantum mechanics leads to the idea that there is randomness and unpredictability at play at the subatomic level of our physical universe. This concept is called indeterminacy, the opposite of Newtonian determinism.

Another notion we hear lots of talk about these days is chaos theory. To my mind this theory is more related to Newtonian physics than to quantum mechanics because, as the great thinker Jules Henri Poincaré prescribes in his book *Science and Method*, "a very small cause which escapes our notice determines a considerable effect that we cannot fail to see, and then we say that the effect is due to chance. If we knew exactly the laws of nature and the situation of the universe at the initial moment, we could predict exactly the situation of that same universe at a succeeding moment." This is an important idea for our discussions in this book. Let me clarify by using a racetrack as an example. If you knew everything about the horses at the time of their race — the weight of the jockeys, the physical health of both the jockeys and the horses, the physical state of the track, how the horses responded to certain ground and weather conditions, etc. — you could predict the outcome of the race. You could call it cosmic handicapping. Chaos theory postulates that if we could see everything, we could, in effect, predict everything that would happen in the future.

Another way of looking at it is that if we could take a cosmic snapshot of every event that affected another event we could predict the outcome of any specific event. A great example of this principle is at play in the stock market. Why do certain stocks go up or down at any given time? Simultaneously a stockbroker in Fredericton needs to cash in some stocks to buy a car, a woman in Victoria puts a buy order in on the basis of a tip about the same stock, an analyst on Wall Street gets nervous about the ability of that stock to perform in the next fiscal quarter, and a mutual fund decides to short itself in a certain industry sector. Now multiply those four events by millions. What appears to be random really isn't. It's just that we can't see all the events that affect this little universe called the stock market.

The above definitions are general and from a lay point of view. I am sure that I have not done these concepts total justice — but you get the idea.

I would now like to move in a little closer to take a more in-depth look at Newtonian physics and the universal law of determinism — the rules of cause and effect.

5

Who's on First?

Let me ask you this: Do things in your life seem to happen suddenly? Think carefully before answering: it is vital to the next idea I want to raise.

When I first asked myself this question, my answer was that in most cases things did not happen suddenly. Upon close investigation, we can easily see that almost nothing happens suddenly — not heart attacks, not business failures, not marital breakups.

Take a heart attack. Bad eating habits create cholesterol buildup, uncontrolled tension and stress raise blood pressure, and so on. Then boom! Many years later a heart attack strikes. It's not hard to see why. But because every event is related to an often long and complex chain of causes and effects, we don't have a clue that these connections exist.

The law of causality states that to every event there can be ascribed a cause — with the exception of the First Cause. It observes that at one level in our physical world nothing happens randomly — for every effect, there is a cause.

This principle of action-reaction is one of the fundamental truths of the Perfect System.

Nothing less than the total comprehension of this truth will suffice. It will prove to be one of the essential elements in your quest for personal success. Yet this important concept of cause and effect is never truly taught at any level of our public education system — not in elementary, secondary, graduate, or post-graduate classrooms. There simply is no class in the world called "Cause and Effect," although this principle, or rather our lack of understanding it, has led us to wage war against our fellow beings for all of recorded history. It has also resulted in our tacit acceptance of the planet's ecological desolation. And, on the personal level, it is directly responsible for the unhappiness, disorder, and discontent that characterize our lives.

Our ignorance is creating misery that deepens like an ocean shelf, worse for each successive generation, both globally and personally. It is the reason why courses in Crisis Mediation and Conflict Resolution are quickly becoming necessary in today's school system. Teachers regularly report that antisocial behaviour in their classrooms has reached epidemic proportions — and a class that is unruly is a class that is unproductive. A class that is unruly is also a potential hotbed of racism, sexism, and other forms of intolerance. In the lower grades, we teach our children the arts, the sciences, the basic learning tools of reading and writing, yet we utterly ignore what is both our greatest responsibility and our greatest opportunity: to influence our children wisely before their misbehaviour escalates to the point that it requires crisis management. Teachers are also victimized by this reality. The stress and frustration that arise from having to deal with this issue is the number-one reason for teacher burnout.

In the secular as well as in the nonsecular world, appropriate human behaviour is usually guided by one of these two universal maxims (which amount to the same injunction):

DO UNTO OTHERS AS YOU WOULD HAVE
THEM DO UNTO YOU, *and* LOVE YOUR
NEIGHBOUR AS YOURSELF.

These are not merely two lofty ideals, high-minded but impractical; they are a precise blueprint for appropriate social behaviour. Just as $E = mc^2$ is a universal truth written as a formula, so are the above injunctions. They make up the ultimate contract between human beings: "I will treat others the way I want to be treated by them." It could hardly be simpler, could it?

Yet this contract is broken or violated every day. Why?

The answer appears to be because no personal gain or loss seems evident in our actions: we don't perceive any cause and effect. Seldom are there repercussions in the moments immediately after we've performed a positive or negative action. We do not see the eventual reward or punishment as tied to the action, because time separates the cause and the effect, thus creating an illusion that the two are not joined. If you were to understand the consequential effects of an action/cause (the reward or the punishment), then you would be more likely to choose positive actions over negative ones. In fact, you'd be crazy not to.

Another reason that this most fundamental of human contracts has gone by the wayside is that we live in a world boiling over with examples of people — many of them in high positions — who violate the principles with apparent impunity. Some of them literally get away with murder. Others cheat on their income taxes, frequently through loopholes or legal cunning. They don't regard their actions as serious, let alone as fraud or the abrogation of social responsibility. Many of us, in many ways, steal from each other. People mentally and physically abuse their spouses and their children. And there is constant injustice in the workplace — the exploitation of minds and bodies that is directly related to the ever-widening and deeply worrying gulf between rich and poor. Daily, we see all this reported in the newspapers, we witness much of it happening live on TV, and we experience it in the often tragic human dramas played out by neighbours, friends, relatives, and even ourselves.

This is the dilemma: we live in a world where choosing for oneself without regard for others is rewarded, often applauded. We live in a "front page" world where negative behaviour and its perpetrators join the pantheon of the cult of celebrity. Fame and notoriety are no longer distinguished from each other. "News" is bad news, and any good news, any positive achievements, are relegated by media to the back pages.

What we are seeing here, however, is not reality. The media present a distorted, short-term view of events. Their purpose is to sell programs or newspapers, which in turn sell advertising, whose cost is determined by audience or circulation figures. It is instant gratification or nothing these days, and the exceptions prove the rule. Our gods have become actors, athletes, filmmakers, even people who are famous for merely being famous, not for actually doing anything.

Yet if we as a society were to expand our list of what is valuable in human endeavour to include such positive traits as sharing, kindness, empathy, and tolerance, we would cause an effect of momentous proportions. This would indeed be a "shot heard around the world." If we could just teach our children that causes and effects are joined, then we wouldn't need school credit courses with names like "Peacemaking" and "Conflict

Resolution" because our actions would always be focused on keeping the peace rather than on moderating conflict. Education in cause and effect would eventually eradicate the need for intercession by removing the cause of conflict at its root.

Failure to grasp the laws of cause and effect creates chaos, in our lives and in our world. To master the principles, however, is to begin the process of mastering our very lives, because the laws of cause and effect apply immutably to all physical matter. Whether we are talking about a tree, an ocean, or a corporate executive, the same laws apply. This is hard science, too, not mysticism; in fact it's embodied in Newton's third law of motion, which states that forces always occur in pairs — that is, for every action there is an equal and opposite reaction. In personal terms this law could be expressed as "you cannot touch without being touched" — and the other way around. Take a moment and think about the profundity of this principle.

There are other laws at play within the above principles: Newtonian mechanics requires that momentum and energy be conserved in collisions. This conservation leads to a balance of momentum and energy in a system. (Consider holding six rubber balls in your hand; if you release them randomly, they all bounce around on the ground, but after a while no ball is moving much faster than any other and they must eventually come to rest and stop moving entirely.) Basically, the principle of conservation of energy taken with the conservation of mass leads to the conclusion that all energy has a need to seek equilibrium or balance. Essentially this means that everything must eventually be in harmony and balance. So through our actions, whatever energy we give or take must return in equal measure.

Science surrounds this issue like Indians circling covered wagons in bad B movies. We have no escape from its apparent truth. Yet we disregard all that we see and know. We keep doing actions that create ill effects for ourselves, our friends, our business associates, and our families.

I keep pushing this point because the law of cause and effect is the prime determining factor in our ability to satisfy our personal needs and desires. Here's a personal anecdote that amply demonstrates the potent truth of this fundamental law.

My mother-in-law, a kind and gentle woman, not the clichéd she-wolf of stand-up comedy, lived with my wife and me for a time after our second son was born. She accepted the invitation to become a permanent member of our family after our house nearly burned down one Christmas Eve. We were in the middle of moving to a new house and found ourselves living out of suitcases in a rented apartment. While I was out all day working and building my business, Ellen, my wife, was at our new house finishing the interior design. Nanna (Ellen's mom's nickname) pitched in to help with our two boys. Jacob was two years old and Isaac was no more than four months. Jake was old enough to be with Ellen during the days, but Isaac stayed home with Nanna.

Fast forward to one year later. We were settled in our new house and getting on with our lives when Nanna had a stroke. She died three weeks later in hospital. Isaac was one and a half when she passed away. By the time he was two and a half, his personality had started to change, subtly at first, then more noticeably. He was becoming increasingly hostile. This hostility grew so intense that when I came home from work Jacob would give me a standing ovation, but Isaac would hit me. If it was almost cute to begin with, it wasn't after a while; Isaac's actions were filled with anger. It escalated to the point that he would not even let anyone hold him. If Ellen or I tried to snuggle him, he would wrench himself away. If no man is an island, my boy was becoming one — with an uncharted ocean surrounding him.

We are a loving family. We don't fight, shout, or vent our hostilities on each other. Ellen and I have consciously and carefully created a safe, respectful environment, both for ourselves and for our children. It is our shelter from the storms of the world, our refuge. So Isaac's actions were out of context. We discussed consulting a child psychologist because, frankly, we were scared. It appeared that Isaac had somehow become "damaged goods," and the problem preoccupied me.

Then the strangest event happened. One night Ellen, the two boys, and I were sitting on our bed watching home videos. There on the TV screen was Nanna by our swimming pool playing with the boys. Isaac — by now all of three and a half years old — jumped off the bed, walked up to the TV, and started to violently slam the cupboard doors below it. It was a stunning revelation to me: obviously, Isaac's anger and withdrawn behaviour were connected with the loss of his grandmother. I never thought until then that such a young child could be moved in such a profound way. He had bonded physically and emotionally with Nanna — of that there was never any doubt — but he was just eighteen months old when she died. Furthermore, after her death, we thought we did everything to ensure that the transition was seamless for him. On every level, his nurturing was the same, if anything even greater than before, because we were self-consciously compensating for Nanna's absence.

Most perplexing, probably, was that we started seeing the signs of Isaac's personality change only a year after Nanna's death. The connection between cause and effect was so subtle and distant, it didn't occur to us to link the two events. Ellen and I had no clue such a storm was brewing, and now that it was thundering over our heads what were we supposed to do?

My anguish must have been obvious to close friends, one of whom eventually asked me what was going on. So I told him the whole story, and when I'd finished he had some advice, which, after a discussion with Ellen, I implemented in the following way.

One night not long after our revelation, I was reading a story to Jacob and Isaac, who sleep in the same room. Jacob was sitting on my lap; Isaac, as usual, was sitting by himself on the other side of the room, eyes downcast, reading his own picture book. By now I'd come to respect this territorial imperative he'd created for himself; it was about all I could do to appease him. However, on this night I suddenly stopped reading the story to Jacob, put the book aside, and started a conversation with Jacob instead — knowing full well that Isaac was listening.

"Jake," I said, "you know what I miss about Nanna the most?"

He replied, "No."

"I really miss the way Nanna used to hug me."

Jacob agreed with this, so I continued. "But I have a great idea. The next time we feel we're missing Nanna, let's give each other a hug exactly the way Nanna used to."

Jacob asked, "What do you mean?"

I pulled him close to me and said, "I'll hug you just like Nanna did."

As I held him close, I could feel Isaac staring at me, so I turned to him and asked, "Would you like me to do the same thing with you when you feel you miss your Nanna?"

He nodded. I moved across the room and sat next to him. Immediately, he clambered up onto my lap and hugged me so hard I could feel the pain pouring out through his little body. He shuddered, heaved, and finally, for the first time in ages, lay at ease in my arms. He had shed most of the sorrow and pain of

Nanna's death and absence in that one moment, although it took many more months of "hugging like Nanna hugged" to completely exorcise his angst and melancholy. Yet before too long, his anger receded, his love shone out again, and his behaviour became that of a normal child.

The whole painful period was for me a crash course in the stark reality in the power of cause and effect.

~

I was one of the lucky ones. If it wasn't for the family-video incident I fear that I would have an emotionally damaged child on my hands today.

We must never forget that people affect us . . . or that we affect people.

Our actions have the power to create positive and negative responses. Understanding this gives us foresight, an ability to see and imagine what will happen when we perform any action. The questions we must ask are: "How will this action affect me?" and "How will this action affect the people around me?"

To further illustrate this point, let me ask you a question: Is there someone in your life you love to be with — say, a favourite uncle, aunt, friend, or grandparent? Then ask yourself why that person is your favourite.

In my case, the person was a woman by the name of Judy Thornley. We were the same age. She was my best friend from the time I was twenty until she died at forty of ovarian cancer. What made her my best friend, aside from all the obvious "relationship stuff" like ultimate trust and the comfort I felt with her, was that I knew she truly loved me, unconditionally. When I walked into her house, her face would light up. She laughed at all my bad jokes, forgave my many foibles. In short, she saw only the best in me. And of course I felt the same about her. We nourished each other. In case you're thinking otherwise, ours was a purely platonic relationship, because it was better than sex and we instinctively knew it.

While researching this book, I sought to verify my own experiences, so I asked the above question of numerous focus groups. Most responded to the question of why their chosen person was so special with such answers as: he made me feel special; she made me feel I could do no wrong; he made me feel good about myself; and so on. Do these answers match your own findings? Does the person you picked make you experience the same feelings? I am pretty certain you've answered in the affirmative.

Another thing I learned from focus groups was that not only did people want to be in their special person's company again and again but they also found themselves giving that person, in return, tremendous kindness and respect.

The point I'm making is that where there is a clearly identifiable cause (in this case your favourite person's positive behaviour), there is also a clearly identifiable effect (your emotional responses of respect and admiration, as well as the ongoing desire to be with that person). This is the purest example of the power of cause and effect: IT WORKS! And, whether you are a person or a corporation, the more sharing and kindness you give others, the more they and the world will respond to you in the same manner. It may seem simple in theory, but you probably know how difficult it can be in practice.

In business, given a situation where price and selection are relatively equal among competitors, the notion of nourishment and sharing can become a singular competitive advantage — in much the same way that, if you want someone to be your friend, kindness, nourishment, and sharing become the key components in building that relationship. This is true only because you have forged a genuine connection to one of the rules of the Perfect System: for every action there is an equal and opposite reaction. Thus, if you think of the other person first and take care of his needs before your own, you must get the same back. It is guaranteed that not only will that person want to be with you — in whatever sense is intended — but he will also want to share with you in return, according to the nature of the arrangement.

In life as well as in business, if an acquaintance doesn't act as if he cares for me and respects me, along with my values and needs, then I will not be interested in having a lasting relationship, or indeed any kind of relationship, with that person or his business. I will withdraw my permission for her to build a relationship with me, and whatever bridges she has built she will also have burned.

Take note of this word *permission*, because within it lies an essential value of all relationships. I will say more on this subject in a coming chapter.

Remember: in any interaction, whatever we get back, it is always our choice because we can control our actions and reactions. If we're destructive, negative, or self-serving, we will reap the same. This too is a part of the same perfect rule of the Perfect System. So the next time you are about to react in a situation, ask yourself "What is it that I want back?" If it isn't what you are giving, you will not get it. And if your answer is "I don't know," then you are not even ready to be in the situation itself.

This may seem like common sense — and it is — but, in your experience, how common a thing is common sense?

The following anonymous story has been circulating on the Internet for several years, and I use it now to illustrate, in a funny way, the power of cause and effect:

INSURANCE CLAIM #233

Dear Sirs,

I am writing in response to your request for additional information. In block #8 on the accident form, I put "Trying to do the job alone" as the major cause of my accident.

You said in your letter that you needed a more detailed report, and I trust the following will be sufficient.

I am an air-conditioning/heater person by trade. On the date of the accident, I was working alone on the roof of a new six-storey building.

When I completed my work, I found that I still had about 500 pounds of tools on the roof. Rather than carry these tools down six flights of stairs by hand, I then decided to lower them from the roof in a barrel by rope and pulleys.

Securing the rope at ground level, I then went up to the roof and swung the barrel out and loaded the tools into the barrel. Then I went back down to ground level and untied the rope, holding it tightly to ensure a slow descent of the 500 pounds of tools.

You will note in block #11 of the accident report that I weigh 135 pounds. You can imagine my surprise when suddenly I was jerked off the ground, lost my presence of mind, and forgot to let go of the rope.

Needless to say, I proceeded at a rather alarming rate up the side of the building. In the vicinity of the third floor, I met the barrel coming down the side of the building. This will explain the fractured skull and broken collarbone.

Slowed only slightly, I continued my rapid ascent, not stopping until the knuckles on my right hand were burned two inches deep into the pulley. Fortunately at this time, I regained my presence of mind and was able to hold on to the rope in spite of the pain.

At approximately the same time, the barrel hit the ground and the bottom fell out of the barrel, dumping the tools into a pile on the ground.

With the barrel now empty — and again I refer you to the block #11 on my weight — I began a rapid descent down the side of the building.

Again in the vicinity of the third floor, I met the barrel coming up. This will explain the two fractured ankles and lacerations on my legs.

When I hit the barrel, it slowed me down enough so that when I fell on the tools, I only sustained three broken vertebrae in my back.

I am sorry to report that as I lay on the ground in pain, I again lost my presence of mind and let go of the rope. The barrel came down and broke my hip.

I hope that this is sufficient information for the insurance company. Please send the cheque to me.

Yours truly,
Murphy S. Law

Cause and effect

6

The Rules of the Game
and the Five Senses

I magine a pristine baseball field. On that field, place your all-
time favourite baseball players — Mickey Mantle, Babe Ruth,
Ty Cobb, Roger Maris, Mark McGwire, Sammy Sosa, whomever.
Now picture these players with the best-looking uniforms, the
best gloves and bats and other equipment. Then imagine the fans
in the stadium anticipating the start of the game.

What would happen if the rules of baseball were not known
to these players? The fans would start booing, the players would
start making their own rules, heated disagreements would arise
over these new rules, fighting would break out, players would
leave the game — maybe to make up a new game — and owners
would be yelling at each other. In short, total chaos. Next, think
of one of the players, say, Mark McGwire, probably one of the
greatest long-ball hitters in baseball history. He always had this
potential, even as a child. Yet his prodigious skill was allowed to
manifest itself only because he found a game to play that had

rules. The game was called baseball. First he learned the rules and then he played.

Each one of us is a potential Mark McGwire in the game of life. Each one of us is born into the world with a prodigious talent. But if we don't know the rules of the game, that talent will remain unrealized. So if we don't know the rules of the game — any game — how can we achieve our potential or even have a chance at winning? Unfortunately most of us are beaten before we start!

This is why it is so very, very important for us to know the rules of the Perfect System — the rules of life. I can't emphasize this imperative enough. If you don't know the rules of the game, forget about winning, you can't even play. You don't have a chance. That's why most of us experience booing from the crowd (disapproval from our mates and co-workers) and chaos (depression, discord, and anxiety), and some of us even leave the game (suicide).

Something stops us from seeing the big picture — the Perfect System. What is it about the human condition that stops us from seeing the truth?

In the big picture, the Perfect System is one of order and balance. But we cannot perceive this order and balance because we are limited by our five senses. Our five senses are the tools we use to filter the physical world's information into our minds. Look at any ecosystem to see how our senses can limit us. If we were to see a lion in the wild killing a zebra, an acceptable interpretation of the event would be that the lion, being stronger, killed a weaker animal, the zebra. A chilling truth, this: the strong overpowering the weak. Yet it is not correct. What our sense of sight registered was limited. If we had big-picture vision we would see that a herd of zebras can move only

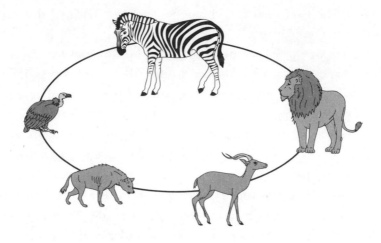

as fast as the slowest zebra, and when the herd is hunted, it is the slowest and weakest ones at the back that are killed first. This natural selection is good for the herd as a whole, because the general speed and health of the whole is maintained by the regular culling of the weakest members.

This weakest member was thus placing the herd in jeopardy, because its migration to the next pasturing or watering place was being retarded by that weaker member. Another thing that we probably did not see was that the lion left a portion of the carcass for scavengers (hyenas, vultures, etc.) to feed on, so that they would have enough strength to weed the weak members out of a pack of gazelles. And so on ad infinitum. We don't see these things because of our five senses, or rather because of their limitations.

These senses tend to overpower us by either shutting down our intuition or making us jump to conclusions. This is neither good nor bad, I must emphasize; it just is. An instant alarm tells us when we are in trouble, but the alarm is often incorrect or mistaken. The way we use our five senses is simply limiting. Our senses do offer us different perspectives on the truth, yet these perspectives are only imperfectly grasped clues to the existence of a higher and absolute truth.

According to the Perfect System, three molecular components make up our universe: the electron, the proton, and the neutron, together known as the atom. In addition, there is a fourth element, the photon, the particle that forms light and acts as a vehicle for the forces that bind the atom together. These four elements form the foundation of our physical world in its entirety. We are all made up of atoms. Tables, cars, people, planets, and stars are all atomic in structure. Physics has taught us that almost all the physical mass of an atom is contained within its nucleus. The rest of the atom is simply space. The relationship between a nucleus — the physical part of an atom — and the rest of the atom is like that of an ant in relation to a football field.

Thus, if we were to condense all of the atoms in a table down to their nuclei or physical mass, the table would practically disappear. This is the reality, yet when we use our five senses to look at the table, we perceive form, mass, and solidity. When we knock on the table, for example, our limited senses tell us that it is solid. We just cannot see the reality of the space within the table. We are limited by touch and sight. But if we did not jump to conclusions and were able to extend the abilities of our five senses, say by using some sort of powerful microscope, we would be able to see another truth, a deeper truth.

There are, of course, many more examples of the restrictive nature of our five senses. Consider electromagnetic waves: five hundred years ago they would have been considered a mystical concept. Radio waves are all around us. Our limited five senses prevent us from seeing them, although when we turn on the radio we hear music. But is it logical to say that because we cannot see the radio waves they don't exist? No. And take music itself, which is simply vibrations in the air that reach the tiny membrane in the ear called the tympanum. There is no scientific explanation whatsoever for why some music makes us think of beer and pretzels while other music elevates our minds to spiritual contemplation. Yet, without being able to offer even a shred of evidence to prove it, not one scientist on the planet would deny that these different experiences happen. Similarly, we know that what we see is sometimes very far from what is actually there. A very bright star, for instance, could in fact be a supernova, an ostensibly dead, burned-out planet. Because light travels at 186,000 miles per second, you could be looking at a star that has been dead for thousands, if not millions, of years.

Let's face it: our senses are not reliable. And limited views will permit only limited intellectual decision-making. If our decisions are limited, then so are our results. And so we generally receive limited happiness and fulfillment from the decisions we make in our lives. How could it be otherwise? Imprisoned by the five senses in a world of illusion, the mind has merely become very adept at guesswork.

In order for us to achieve total fulfillment and happiness, we must have a total view of reality. What is required is nothing less than a complete picture of our universe, a comprehensive understanding of how things work. Our five senses tap only results, manifestations, or effects. Seldom do they tap the causes behind these effects. For example, every tree has a cause, which is what, literally and metaphorically, we call a seed. Our five senses, however, don't see this: they are not geared to tap this seed level, this causal level where the actual exists within the latent. Under normal conditions we are unable to see the long, polymorphic process of a seed transforming itself into a tree because the seed is hidden from our sense of sight.

The opposite happens when our limited five senses become overloaded with information — with sounds, smells, images, tastes, and touch. Under such conditions, our systems can even shut down, ignoring excess information in order to perform some limited task. In the simple act of crossing a street, for instance, there is all manner of sensory information that the brain will decide to filter out because it is not contextually relevant at that moment. Birds are chirping, children shouting, leaves rustling, mouth-watering aromas are wafting from hot-dog vendors' carts. Yet we are not aware of all of this sensory symphony because our minds are focused solely on what we believe to be relevant: the sound of car tires screeching to a halt, for example, or a horn honking, or a child's footsteps running into the street.

The theory of chaos is another validator of our physical limitations. Remember that it was expressed in the idea that the universe behaves like a single entity in which the many parts are linked to each other and the whole governed by one immutable law of causality (the law of causality states that to every event there can be ascribed a cause, with the exception of the First Cause). Indeed, the new science postulates that everything in the universe, regardless of distance or dissimilarity, is somehow all integrally connected, having emanated from a single source.

This concept is not surprising from any system originating from a single cause. As stated earlier, the unfortunate part of this unified causal paradigm is that effects are often far removed in appearance from their causes, and what seems to occur for no reason is in reality the consequence of a specific event, cataclysmic or trivial. The causal universe — the place deep within the physical form, and from whence that form originated — is the ultimate material reality. Our inability to see the forest for the trees, to see the real for the illusory, is thus directly related to the limitations of our senses, which encourage specialization rather than holistic thought.

Let me now show you how to go beyond these five senses, how to see the big picture by using the Perfect System.

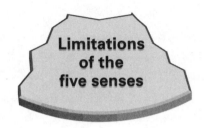

7

What Do You Want Out of Life?

Consider this story:

An American businessman was at the pier of a little village on the Mexican coast when a small boat with just one fisherman docked. Inside the boat were several large yellowfin tuna. The American complimented the skipper on the quality of his fish and asked how long it had taken to catch them.

"Señor," the grizzled old skipper replied, "I stay out only a little while . . . maybe five or six hours."

The American then asked the man why he didn't stay out longer and catch more fish.

"But, Señor, I have enough for my family and what they need today" was the reply.

"But what do you do with the rest of your time?"

"I sleep late, fish a little, play with my niños, take siesta with my wife, and stroll into the village each evening to sip wine and play guitar with my amigos. I have a full and busy life, Señor."

The American scoffed. "I'm a Harvard MBA, and I could help you. You should spend more time fishing and with the proceeds buy a bigger boat. With the increased earnings from the bigger boat you could buy several boats, and eventually you would have a fleet of fishing boats. Instead of selling your catch to a middleman, you would sell directly to the processor, eventually opening your own cannery. You would control the product, processing, and distribution. Of course, you would need to leave this village and move to Mexico City, then L.A. and eventually New York City, where you'd run your fishing empire."

"But, Señor, how long will all this take?" asked the skipper.

"Oh, maybe fifteen or twenty years."

"But what then, Señor?"

The American laughed and said, "That's the best part. When the time is right, you would announce an IPO — an initial public offering — sell your company stock to the public, and become very rich. You would make millions and millions."

"Millions, Señor? Then what?"

"Then you could retire," announced the American jubilantly. "You'd move to a small coastal village, sleep late, fish a little, play with your kids, take siesta with your wife, stroll to the village in the evenings and sip wine and play guitar with your amigos."

"But, Señor, I am doing that already."

~

What are we working for? Why do we get married, have kids, pay mortgages? Putting aside sheer survival, of course, what the hell are we doing all this for?

Take a minute to list the things you think would make you happy.

Can you weigh the answers you've given, can you hold them

in your hand? Is there anything on your list that you can even locate in physical space? Again, in most cases when I have asked this question in the seminars I conduct, the answer is usually no. The list usually reads: achieving my potential, financial security, a place of protection (a home), independence, time to do what I want, and so on. Occasionally people respond with money, or a house or a good-looking mate, but with further investigation it wasn't money that the person wanted, or a mate or a house, but the way those things would make him or her feel. Money equalled security or independence. And nobody wants a house — a bricks and mortar edifice — but a *home*, a place of personal, physical, and emotional asylum and protection.

When all of us get down to the truth of this issue, our answers are usually about feelings — feeling secure, feeling good about ourselves, feeling empowered. And all these answers go back to our elemental need to feel filled and not empty. When we feel filled we feel whole and happy, and when we feel empty we feel incomplete and sad. For the purpose of this discussion, I will call this feeling of being totally filled "fulfillment."

And all this leads us to another of the rules of the system: everything that we truly want to receive in our lives is of a non-physical nature. What we really want, as I've said, is to feel fulfilled. Yet most of us imagine that material things will bring happiness, so we become motivated to acquire physical objects — when, as we have seen, the opposite should be our goal. Material things will never satisfy us: it is what material things make us feel that matters.

Haven't we all thought, at some point in our lives, that another car or a different mate or more clothes would bring us happiness? Certainly more money would fix everything! But if any of you have managed to get all or some of these, you now know that it wasn't really true, was it? You weren't any happier.

It was just the same old you with a new mate, more money, or another car. As is often said, no matter where you go, there you are!

A person buys a car. She really wants this car. What happens a week after she purchases it? The satisfaction never equals the expectation, does it? That's because it isn't the car that this person really needs. It is the way the car will make her feel. Once we understand that what we want in life is not money or physical objects but this feeling of fulfillment, we can take advantage of the many opportunities for true, sustainable fulfillment that exist in our lives. This is no simple task. The hardest thing to do is to identify in the thick of an experience why we are in that experience in the first place. I am overweight. I buy food and eat large quantities at supper because it makes me feel full. But every morning I get up feeling empty again. It wasn't about the food for me. It was about my feeling empty inside. Once I realized the dynamics of the situation, I was able to try to discover longer-lasting, more sustainable remedies for fulfillment.

I will discuss this whole fascinating subject in greater detail in an upcoming chapter. For now, consider the notion that every one of us feels empty at some point in our daily, weekly, and monthly lives and we will do the craziest things to get rid of this feeling. Some of us overeat, some take drugs, others change mates, others become sexually promiscuous, and some go on shopping sprees. Unfortunately these all feel good at the time of fulfillment, but we do ourselves enormous damage when we go for *short-term* fulfillment. This fulfillment doesn't last long, and we are driven to keep the feeling going. Short-term solutions, unfortunately, equal guilt, emotional and physical pain, and more feelings of emptiness. There is no happy ending to any substance addiction (food, drugs, etc.), no happy endings to any short-term solutions. But we all need to feel fulfilled and we will do almost anything to achieve it — even for five minutes!

Being full-fledged students of the Perfect System, we must now ask ourselves the one and only pertinent question: Why? Why is it that all we really want out of life is fulfillment? For the answer, we must go back to the First Cause. Do you remember its attributes? Let me refresh your memory. The Big Bang was an explosion, not an implosion, a movement outward, not inward. It kept nothing back for itself. But there is one other key element of the First Cause.

The First Cause at the moment of Creation was a singularity that was total and complete. Just as we have a relationship with the concept of cause and effect, we have an affinity with the completeness of the First Cause. We seek true, long-lasting fulfillment, because, linked to the First Cause as we are, it is our nature, too.

It is essential to remember that the First Cause was without lack (was complete) and then it exploded, keeping nothing back for itself. This is all we truly know about the condition of the First Cause and its behaviour at the point of physical creation.

Let's now continue on this theme of fulfillment. Make a list of those things that make you unhappy or dissatisfied with your life: a poor relationship with your boss or lover, difficulties with your kids, lack of financial security, and so on. Keep referring to your list as we continue, because soon you will find that its contents are clues to the areas in your life where you are not dealing with your affinity with the First Cause or you are in violation of some other rule or principle of the Perfect System.

Selfless Selfishness

By now you have seen that the laws of cause and effect and the principles of fulfillment are very powerful indeed, with the potential for good and for bad. We must be careful in all our dealings. As stated in the previous chapter, because of our affinity with the First Cause we all need to feel fulfilled. Yet we are all conditioned by our society to pursue short-term fulfillment. We are inundated with this message at an early age from the attitudes and behaviour of our parents and school friends and the advertising we see and hear all around us. There is no fault here. It just is. Discussion about the reason for this state is counterproductive. The fact is that we live in a culture of consumerism where the driving message is consume and be happy. (Cynically, the eventual upside to this premise will probably be world peace because it is just bad business to kill consumers.)

The problem with being conditioned to pursue short-term fulfillment is that it always results in long-term losses. Sarcasm, anger, violence, vengefulness, promiscuous sex, and drugs all feel good for the moment because of our basic need for fulfill-ment. But that feeling is short-lived and ends up causing us harm. Just picture the repercussions that inevitably follow any of the above reactive responses: nothing remotely good can come from them in the long run. It feels good at the moment to scream at someone who is acting like an idiot, but the conse-quences are disconnection from that person. If you are a macho guy, it feels great to take a swing at someone who is annoying the hell out of you, but the consequence could be physical injury to you or another person or criminal charges or a lawsuit.

Think about what it is you really want to see returning to you as a consequence of your actions. A cruel putdown might make you feel good or powerful for a moment, but never lose sight of what you — of what we all — really want out of life: true, lasting fulfillment.

Will your next action get you what you really want?

This is really about enabling good things to happen in our lives, as opposed to negative things. The bad news is that nothing less than an absolute understanding of this rule will assist you in changing your life. But, as always, there's good news, too: the rule is very simple indeed. We can control most things that happen to us by an action that we do or, paradoxically, by some-thing that we don't do. I said "most things" because we can influence only what happens to *us* — not what happens to *others*. For example, often we have no influence over the health of loved ones. Their sickness or dying brings us great pain. The knowledge contained in the Perfect System allows us to under-stand the dynamic of the experience we are going through and helps us get on with our lives while dealing with the pain of loss. As we learn the rules, we gain more control and, heart-breakingly, we also come to understand why what happens to other people is out of our hands.

Remember, on the grand scale, we are ultimately responsible for our own actions — and the reactions that come back to us. Thus, for every action that you perform, you have nobody but yourself to thank or to blame for the effect it causes. It is of course easier to blame others, but it is not just, it is not right. Historically we are conditioned as humans to blame the weather, our mates, our bosses, the banks, the immigrants, whatever, for our lack of feeling fulfilled. Instinctively, we see that we have something and they want to take it away from us. Blaming others is a knee-jerk response mechanism rooted in our fear of lacking something or, depending how you look at it, of not being fulfilled.

So, although our very socialized nature rebels against taking responsibility for all that happens to us, we must change that nature. Even when we don't see any cause-and-effect link, we must remind ourselves that it is always present, always in play. Every action — good, bad, ugly, or indifferent — generates a consequence, a reaction, according to its nature. This is a major component in the basic laws of physics, but it's also a rule that affects us. Never forget that this system is perfect. It is not arbitrary and it doesn't make mistakes.

It is important to note that this principle transcends concepts like selfishness and selflessness or any negative judgment surrounding the idea of manipulating others for your own benefit. The term *selfishness* has had an unjustly bad press over the last thousand-odd years. In reality, being selfish is essential to changing your life. Let me clarify what I mean by selfish, though: it has to do with what we really need, not what we think we want. Remember, it wasn't material goods that we needed, it was something else, something we couldn't hold in our hands — it was true and lasting fulfillment. And it's logical that we would do anything to get what we desire avidly. Yet the trouble is that we go about getting it the wrong way. Losing tempers, escaping into drugs, wallowing in loveless sex, plotting dire revenge — these don't work because they are just like vials of air when what we need is the whole sky. And *need* is the word. This is where selfishness comes in: it is an absolute truth of human nature that we literally need — just as we need air, water, and food — the energy that is fulfillment. And we will do anything to get it. Don't get hung up on putting a moralistic value on it. Judgment lengthens our journey needlessly. Truths are neither good nor bad. They just have to be dealt with. The more you understand this idea, the more empowered you will be.

But because life appears so maddeningly complex, you're probably asking, "How do I react in a situation that isn't black and white, when I don't know what to do?"

When I am unsure of what to do in a situation, I ask myself two questions before I react. First, "How would I want to be treated in the same situation?" And then, "What good will it do?"

What good will it do? Accent on the *good*. And the good must be to others first, not to yourself. Will your action help the other person? Will it be constructive or destructive? If the focus is not on the other person then you could say, "Going berserk will make me feel good," or "Giving that person the cold shoulder is just what he deserves and that's good." Get the picture? Going berserk only leads to short-lived fulfillment and plenty of trouble afterwards, just as a refusal to acknowledge another person can lead to more disconnection, frustration, and resentment. Nothing good can come from an action that is not focused first on the betterment of another person. We all want to be treated with respect, forgiveness, and compassion.

I ask myself these questions because I want to control my life and the things that happen to me. And I know, beyond all doubt, that good gets good back — and vice versa.

Here's a business example of this principle in action. In the mid-eighties I had an idea to buy old Japanese TV footage and re-record the audio track with funny voices and narrative, just as Woody Allen did in his first film, *What's Up, Tiger Lily?* I wanted to find a Japanese science fiction show from the sixties and from it create an original TV comedy series. I started my research and discovered that acting with honour was an important aspect of Japanese culture. However, I also learned that negotiating with the Japanese at that time was very difficult, and even if you managed to make a deal it took forever to consummate legally, let alone get delivery of the product. But off I went to Japan anyway, in search of my footage and confident that I had the right negotiating tools to bypass the traditional way Japanese business with the West was done.

~

It may sound crazy, but after a while of seeing the potency of the Perfect System in action, you build a confidence in handling difficult situations that formerly you'd have been unjustified in having. While doing my homework before setting out, I'd discovered that most North Americans' negotiations were biased because of their history in dealing with the Japanese. Usually what happened was that the two parties would get together and socialize, and socialize, and socialize some more — until the foreigners' time was running out. Then and only then would the Japanese start to discuss business, knowing full well that they held the leverage in negotiations because the other party had to return home. It was at this point that negotiations became fast, furious, and even emotional. The Americans tried a hardball approach to knock down the original price. But the Japanese would respond with a still higher price, and so the negotiating spiral continued. I also found out that, a year earlier, another entertainment company had bought rights under similar conditions and ended up paying around $200,000 for a two-year package of fifty-two shows.

So there I was in Japan. I managed to find exactly the show and footage I needed, and I started to negotiate with the Japanese. Immediately, they suggested that we all go out to eat and talk over supper — just as I anticipated they would.

"No, thank you," I told them. "I've come here to find my material and negotiate a contract for its use for five years exclusive. I am not prepared to negotiate price with you. Whatever you think is fair for you will be fine with me as long as I can afford it." As I was leaving the head honcho's office, I added, "Listen, I instinctively know that you are an honourable man and I trust that you will be fair with me . . . So please call me in the morning with your price."

I was taking no risk in negotiating like this. I could always refuse if the price was too dear. But my action disarmed the Japanese because I'd put the responsibility of price and honour on their shoulders. I knew they would be fair — and they were. The head honcho called me the next morning with a price of $65,000 for *five* years for fifty-two shows. The contract was written and executed in two days, and I was on my way home with a great deal both for me and the Japanese. I was a satisfied buyer because I had had the will to create a satisfied seller.

Now let's examine the powerful dynamics of what happened in this deal as I used the Perfect System. I had to make a decision walking into the negotiation that I would not play according to the other party's rules, because from my research I saw that his rules inevitably led either to an unsatisfied buyer or an unsatisfied seller. To change the rules, I decided that I would never back him into a corner during our discussions. I knew he was an expert at fighting his way out of corners. I gave him the whole room and he found he was the only person in it. I forced him to change his interaction with me. However, the key part of this successful transaction was that I really meant what I said and I said what I meant. With all my heart, I really wanted him to feel that he had gotten a fair deal for himself, that I wasn't there to screw him, nor was I there to get the cheapest deal. I was there to protect his interest before my own. Armed with such a consciousness and certainty, I couldn't lose. And haven't since then.

~

Are you starting to get it? The rules of the system are perfect. The sun doesn't forget to rise in the morning, and spring always comes before summer. From stars to atoms, the same laws apply, the same system governs — and that system states that the more sharing you do, the more you get back in return. For every action there is an equal and opposite reaction.

9

Planting

Now that you are gaining more insight into the concept of power of cause and effect and fulfillment, let me ask you this question: Is there an example in nature that is a metaphor for the beginning of all potentiality? You could answer that the very beginning, when the First Cause was a singularity, could be considered the beginning of potentiality. Another example might be the moment of conception of a child. I would like to focus on a simpler, more explicit illustration.

Where is the "all" of a tree? Where is it decided how many branches the tree is going to have, how much fruit it will bear, how long it will live, what the fragrance of its flowers will be?

It all exists, in potential, within the seed. That is why it is critical, when we are at a time of creating a seed — as we are when creating a new business or entering into new personal relationships of any kind — that we be conscious of the thought and will that go into their beginnings. From the seed comes the tree — irrevocably. In all matters, the desire for unity and true sharing must be in the seed if we are hoping for any kind of long-term fulfillment coming from it. When greed or unbalanced self-interest play a part in this beginning, what sprouts from the seed will not last long. The plant is basically doomed from the start.

This is another fundamental rule of the Perfect System: we are most potent when we are creating new friendships or business opportunities — not in the midst of business or personal relationships but at the very beginning of those relationships.

Here is my own business experience: whenever I created a partnership with someone who, say, I knew was greedy, I usually made short-term money, but in the long run I always lost more than I made. And, finally, the parting wasn't so much a sweet sorrow as it was an expensive and acrimonious one. Shakespeare knew a lot about love but little about business. When I created a seed in the wrong state of consciousness, I inevitably lost out — I wasted time and money. This was an important lesson for me, and it should also be one for you. The law involved — like every other law of the Perfect System — is straightforward and easy to understand, yet it can be so difficult to implement, largely because we tend to be either too greedy or else too impetuous to control our behaviour.

Whereas business costs time and money, personal relationships are more psychologically and physically expensive because there's usually a lot more emotional debris flying around. Angry spouses and hurt and disenfranchised children are all major victims of thoughtless seed creation.

For example, two people marry, but their relationship is not based on common values and the philosophy of ultimate sharing (literally putting a partner's needs before your own). As we know from the laws of cause and effect, this behaviour is the only way to get what we really want out of life — true, long-lasting fulfillment. Result: that relationship, unfortunately, is doomed. It will not endure. Guaranteed! An inappropriately seeded relationship will also eventually leave emotionally scarred children and emotionally damaged adults. It will result in a mess. Yet we continually put ourselves in relationships that will wither and die, don't we? This is unfortunate, to say the least, because the principle involved is one of the easiest to understand and to follow.

Don't marry someone because they make you feel completed (which is different from making you feel fulfilled) or because they are your method of escape from a life of unhappiness and misery. Don't marry someone because you are lonely. Don't marry someone who does not share the same spiritual, moral, and ethical values as you. Don't marry someone who cannot learn to put your needs before their own — if they can't, there will be no nourishment within the seed to foster long-term fulfillment or to support emotionally healthy children. Why? Because those relationships are disconnected from the affinity relationship that we all have with the First Cause. Seeds need systemic nourishment to grow and prosper. If they don't have it they will wither and die.

The other principle at play here is Newton's law of attraction (matter attracts matter, anti-matter attracts anti-matter). What appear to be opposites attracting in relationships is, in my experience, not the case. Yes, there may be differences in personality traits, but if you dig deep enough you will see that partners in healthy, long-lasting relationships share, to some degree, common values, common goals, common points of view, and common interests.

So if you enter a relationship respecting these laws, then the fruits of such a union will be fragrant, wholesome, and healthy, and they'll last a lifetime. The offspring of such a relationship will be emotionally healthy because they will treat each other, their friends, and eventually their own mates by the example of their parents. If you need validation of this principle, make note of the business and personal relationships that you see have been successful over a long time. Ask how they started, what the frame of reference for their beginning was, and you'll inevitably see a commitment to mutual sharing and the embracing of similar values and goals.

Think of the personal and business relationships in your life that have worked and those that have not. See if this "seed" principle resonates with those experiences. Be honest and ask yourself whether there were signs in the bad ones that should have set off alarm bells? Were there signs in the good ones that intuitively made you feel you were on the right track? Divide your list into good experiences and bad experiences.

~

I'm aware that some of what I've said may sound unkind and may be difficult to accept. Granted, it is always tempting to give in to short-term temptations — the quick buck, the intoxication of passionate romance, etc. But we have all had to learn the hard way to create healthy seeds. It is a rule that is irresponsible and frankly self-defeating to ignore. If you want to be successful in personal or business relationships, you must adhere to this law. The refutation of this law will eventually lead to pain for you and for others. Don't be a carrier, be the cure.

If you stick your finger in an electrical outlet and you get a shock, it is not that the electricity is punishing you. It is just a law of the universe that states: if you stick your finger in an electrical outlet you will get a shock and it will hurt. So if you are averse to pain don't stick your finger in an electrical outlet!

~

I've been forced to admit this truth in my own relationships. In my twenties and early thirties, I had many live-in relationships with women, and they all ended in disaster — although I wasn't the one to leave. The women all left me. In retrospect, I can see that they had little choice. I just couldn't get it right. And talk about pain! I remember being so lonely between love affairs that I would have paid a woman money just to lie next to me — not for sex, but just to have the warmth of another body beside me. On the macro level, loneliness is a killer — perhaps the most vicious killer of all.

A psychiatrist friend told me once that he believed that putting any mentally and emotionally healthy person into an isolation cell would lead that person to insanity. Many rationales explain this outcome. Here are the two that make the most sense to me and my life experiences. The first is that human beings are basically social animals that need human interaction to validate and verify their self-images. (I will discuss this concept in a later chapter.) The second is our need for nourishment. However, much of the nourishment we receive comes from human contact and experience. We also know now that we understand the word *nourishment* to be a code word for feeling filled, what we call fulfillment. Loneliness is so excruciatingly painful because it makes us feel not filled. When there is no or little social interaction we become disconnected from a major source of what we all crave, long-lasting fulfillment.

The subject of loneliness is quite complex and filled with nuance and subtlety. I could be flippant and say that the cure for loneliness is get a friend, but that's like saying the cure for insomnia is to get a good night's sleep. When I was in my time of loneliness, I went out and tried to make friends. The problem was they didn't want to "play" with me. You see, I could have been with people but I chose not to because I didn't want to be with people who I felt didn't want to be with me. So by choice I remained lonely. Another example of the nuances surrounding this issue was my aunt. She was in a second marriage for thirty-seven years and confided to me that during all her married life she felt lonely. It is possible to be in a relationship and still feel alone.

However, from my own life experience with aging family members, I can tell you one thing with certainty. There comes a moment within the experience of loneliness when either time or circumstance can force a dangerous disassociation from a fundamental life reality. My opinion is based on the scientific principle that in our physical universe our planet, along with other planets, revolves around the sun. We are not the centre of the universe but an interactive player within a group of orbiting bodies that operate in a mutually cooperative system. This basic fact of astronomy is also the perfect metaphor for successful human interaction and socialization.

Loneliness can create pathology, a dissociation from that truth. When this flashpoint ignites, the opposite can become a lonely person's new reality. He starts to believe that the world and its inhabitants revolve around him. She becomes the sun of her own universe. Tragically, this view in turn leads to more loneliness because his or her needs, viewpoints, words, and actions (which are now totally self-interested and self-focused) become unattractive and in some cases unacceptable to their family and friends. The truth is, as we have seen, we all have a need to be around people who nourish us. Regrettably the reverse is also true. None of us wants to be around a person who takes away from our fulfillment and returns no fulfillment. What exacerbates the situation even more is that the longer this pathology lasts the harder it is to extricate people from their irrational new reality.

Perhaps just recognizing and acknowledging the dynamics of loneliness is a good enough start for us. We may not know what to do but we do know the why of it.

On the micro level, as we dig deeper into this subject we see that the need for intimate physical companionship is just as intense and complex. Having a partner is such an integral part of the human experience that we'll do almost anything to achieve it. Again, we need always to understand that we feel this desire because of our affinity with the First Cause — which was complete and lacked nothing. The First Cause was unity. In its singularity, it was and had everything. This is where our voracious desire for union with another person comes from. We can't abide the emptiness we feel without a mate. We need to feel complete. Being alone is contrary to our affinity with the First Cause.

What can we do to get to this state of completeness? Here's what I have learned. A key necessity for any relationship to thrive and endure is to ensure that its seed contains the characteristics of the First Cause. If proper alignment of self-interest and non-self-interest and the consciousness of unity are not components of the seed, then failure is inevitable.

~

In my case, at the age of thirty-four I found myself very rich, very successful . . . and very, very lonely. I may have been a big success in business, but I was a total failure when it came to personal relationships. I actually thought of hiring a geisha from Japan. At least, I reasoned, it would be an honest relationship, and I would always know where I stood. That's pathetic, I know, but you can see just how damaged and hurt I felt in the wake of my previous relationships.

Yet all the women I'd been involved with were everything I

thought I wanted: beautiful, intelligent, with successful careers of their own. The problem was me. I just didn't know how to love them successfully — and they never taught me how to love back. I was caught in the vortex of a Catch-22, or so it seemed.

The truth, I came to see, was that I was totally self-absorbed and, worse still, I was blaming my girlfriends for *my* failure to take responsibility for my life. I found myself getting in and out of relationships with different women, but the scenarios were always the same: I was always attracted to independent women who all inevitably reverted to acting like little girls when they got behind closed doors. Their independence was an act or didn't hold up to the strength and power of my personality. According to them, they "withered in my shadow." Hearing this complaint from girlfriend after girlfriend became disconcerting and then predictable. I felt beaten because I didn't know how to reduce myself to save the relationships.

The weird part was that I continued to be attracted to the same kind of personality and never saw my pattern of repetitive failure. These women were right, by the way: I was totally self-involved and planted all the wrong ingredients in my relationship seeds. We never had a chance. It's too bad I didn't know about the Perfect System when I was younger. I could have saved those wonderful women and myself a lot of time and aggravation. At that time, all I was feeling after all those bungled relationships was pain and fear. After each failure more scar tissue grew on my heart, and it was becoming hardened. I lived alone for several years out of sheer self-preservation. You can imagine the level of pain I was going through to drive me away from my innate need for human companionship. I was in total despair.

Fortunately, it was at this point in my life that I met my wife, Ellen. To illustrate how cynical I was at the time, I confess that the only reason I proposed to her was that I had turned thirty-six and I felt it was now the time for me to have children. I had enough money to focus on them and, oh yes, I thought she would make a good mother. I am exposing this truth to you because I want you to know how depraved, insensitive and frightened a person can act when not knowing the rules of the game, the rules of life. I was so out of it I decided that when I eventually picked a mate, it would be the result of a totally intellectual decision.

So I created two criteria. The first was that I would not pick a candidate that I was "in love" with. The second was that she would be a meritorious person. I wanted a person I could wake up beside twenty years in the future and still find attractive, admirable, and interesting. I wasn't good at the love thing so I figured if I chose someone with worthy qualities I'd be way ahead of the game.

I wasn't stupid, just crazy. By setting these criteria, I was inadvertently creating a seed with ingredients that actually gave this relationship a chance to succeed. I didn't care if she loved me. I just wanted to be with someone who was a decent, intelligent person and with whom I could make a good life. My receiving expectations were low and my giving desires were high. Ellen, on the other hand, put the same ingredients into her relationship seed with me. We had both created an environment of opportunity for growth and fulfillment. But I am getting ahead of myself. Let me tell you more about Ellen Kessler.

I first met Ellen at an advertising agency. She was one of Canada's first successful women copywriters. She had hired me to write a jingle for her client. She fit my criteria profile perfectly, so one thing led to another — as these things tend to — and there I was four months later asking her to sign a prenuptial

agreement as a condition of our marriage. For some unfath-
omable reason, she agreed, and thus began my married life.

Ellen had a few idiosyncrasies of her own, and she had a
right to them, given the warehouseful she'd married. She didn't
talk much, for example. She found great pleasure in doing
things, but not much pleasure in talking about them. Yet
I came to see that in everything she did, she injected a consciousness of sharing. She rarely talked about the way she felt,
but instead demonstrated her feelings with her actions. I always
knew where I stood with her by what she did. They weren't dramatic gestures, but in their quiet way they drove home her
point like jackhammers on hardened pavement. For example,
every morning when I awoke she brought a cup of tea to me in
bed; and when I came home from work, she always asked me
if I needed something. It wasn't romantic or sloppy: she just
kept asking what she could do for me. And before long, I was
infected with her behaviour.

I started asking what I could do for her. I even started to
think about what she might want before I thought about
myself. This wasn't me, I decided — but what the hell! She was
doing it for me, and doing it for her just made me feel good.
So I carried on, never thinking about what was happening in
any but the most basic, mundane terms. Thus, before I knew it,
Ellen, in her own unique way, had started to teach me how to
love, with her *actions*, not with her words.

Gradually, I began to change, and the relationship also
started to change. My feelings of admiration and respect were
transformed into one of deep love and cherishing: Ellen had
literally saved my life, I realized, and I treasured her for freeing
me. The jackhammer of love that she was wielding was breaking
up the hardness in my heart. She also had this incredible ability
to be in tune with her surroundings. She had an affinity for

nature and nurture, food and flowers, seedtime and harvest, our home and all who entered it, and our children. She became a living example of every principle expressed in this book.

She is how I began to know that true, long-lasting fulfillment was possible. She is why I believe that we should all have hope. She is why I was able to see and grasp the potency of the Perfect System.

She has been my teacher, and by her example has allowed me in turn to develop the ability to show others the art of the possible. Ellen understood the principles of the Perfect System intuitively — I did not. She gave me the confidence to chronicle its subtle intricacies and share that information with you. I recognized that since knowing her, all that I have discovered could fill a book. And this is that book.

**Everything is
in the seed**

10

Restriction

Travel back to your elementary school days. It's time for science class and the lesson today is on the fundamentals of what makes a light bulb work. Can you recall the explanation? If not, let me remind you, because the principles and laws that are at play in the creation of light in a light bulb will become one of your most valued tools for control, certainty, and self-fulfillment.

The positive-voltage side of the circuit (that is, the source of power) drives a positive current through the filament towards the negative-voltage side of the circuit. A positive-voltage side is defined as the side of the circuit with the higher electrical energy, and the negative-voltage side is defined as the side with lesser electrical energy. There is a tendency in nature for the greater to flow to the lesser, with the object being equality and balance. Locks in a river system work on this principle.

Now take a look at the light bulb and see the filament inside the bulb. This filament acts as a resistor to the current flowing in the bulb. The more the filament restricts the flow of the current, the more power and the more light are radiated from the bulb. The filament offers a retarding force to the current, pushing the positive-voltage side and the negative-voltage side back from each other. The filament, as if with arms stretched out at its side, is holding back these two forces and is shouting, "Don't touch, don't touch!" This process creates continuous light — and light, of course, has always been the great, abiding metaphor of long-lasting fulfillment.

Where there is darkness (lack of light) there is no fulfillment and only emptiness. And without restriction there cannot be any sustaining light. We can learn many things from this universal rule. If we think of ourselves as the filaments that push back positive and negative currents, we would potentially be able to create continuous light, or, in our terms, long-lasting fulfillment. The reason, by the way, that we don't want the two opposing currents to touch is that that event will create light, but only for a moment. Usually, that light is a dangerous explosion. As an example, if you have ever had trouble with a dead car battery, you have used those cables that attach to another car battery to boost your dead one. What happens when you accidentally touch the positive end and the negative end of the booster cables? Sparks, right? This illustrates precisely what happens when you deal with opposite energy forces without a restrictor.

Let me give you another personal anecdote to illustrate this principle. A number of years ago I was put in charge of a very substantial project, and my partner suggested it would be wise to appoint someone as a go-between between him and me. When the day came for me to meet this man officially, he walked into my office and shook my hand, and we sat down on chairs no more then four feet apart. He was a small man, I thought, far shorter than I'd imagined he'd be. This somehow added to the incongruity of what he had to say.

"Syd," he began the moment he was seated, "as far as I'm concerned, I'm the new boss around here and I want you to know that it's my way or the highway."

Now, you have to appreciate the fact that I grew up in Hamilton, Ontario. Hamilton isn't Toronto; it's grimier and tougher — and my father was a truck driver, not a dentist or portfolio manager. We were a lower-income family, and went lower still when my father died. I failed grade ten three times, and thus was forced to make my way in the world by any means available. I had been a labourer for five years, and I had built everything I had, up to and including my partnership with Labatt, by the sweat of my brow and my innate business and creative talents. Don't misunderstand me, I had a lot of help from some pretty remarkable employees, top-notch production partners, and a very special man who became my dear lifelong friend and operating partner, Salim Sachedina. But the point is that no one ever gave me a cent — and if my business was now a roaring success, it was because I had the will and intelligence to make it happen. What's more, the business was founded on my vision, and it thrived on the enormous amount of hard work put in by me and others who'd been with me almost since the beginning. I hadn't even taken a holiday in seven years. So you can imagine what was going through my head when I suddenly found this new guy sitting in my office and telling me it was his way or the highway.

Two things occurred to me as viable responses to this rudeness and aggression. The first thought — I kid you not — was that I should reach over, grab his shirt, and kick the living daylights out of him. The second thought was to excuse myself, get my partner on the phone, and politely instruct him to get this idiot out of my office — if not out of the business altogether.

But this incident took place exactly one day after I had first learned about the cosmic rule of restriction at an evening class I was taking. I told myself: "Here's a perfect opportunity to test this alleged universal principle." Like you, probably, I was unsure whether such principles could really effect any meaningful change in my life or in my work. But I decided to take a chance and use the rare opportunity the moment provided. Thus I passed on options one and two and proceeded directly to restriction.

I shut down my physical system — no thinking, no action, no speaking, no nothing. In essence, I did not react. After shutting down completely and going through one other process (I will discuss the technique in greater depth shortly), these words came out of my mouth.

I asked the man, "Do I know you?"

"Why do you ask?" he replied, still aggressive.

"Because I must have offended you sometime in the past, that's why. And I want to apologize to you."

"No, I have never met you," he went on, his tone now very different. "But I want you to know that I have followed your career and I'm a big fan of yours. Why did you ask if you had ever offended me?"

"Well, this is what you just said to me" — I repeated his opening salvo — "so I thought you might be angry at me."

He gasped, as if shocked. "Did I say that? You know, I have a problem with that sort of thing. Sometimes what comes out of my mouth is not what I am feeling, and a lot of people misunderstand me. Thank you so much for pointing it out. What I really meant to say is that I hope that you will consider me an ally and a friend here."

And this is the whole truth and nothing but the truth: from that moment on, this guy became my champion. In fact, he championed the very completion of my vision. And every time we met, he was careful to say precisely what he meant and felt — so much so that we had a beautiful, respectful, nonjudgmental, and near-ideal relationship from that moment on.

Even now, I scarcely dare imagine what would have happened had I chosen either of my first two reactive options. If I had slugged him, I'm sure he would have pressed criminal charges against me at the worst. At the least, he would have become my corporate enemy and blocked the fruition of my vision. If I had chosen to call my partner, I am sure he would have thought, "Kessler can't handle my choice of executives. Syd may be a smart guy but I need a leader who can function in a corporate environment and the last thing in the world I need is another problem. I want my leaders to be proactive." Had I not picked the restriction route, I would, by my own hand, have doomed my relationship with my partner.

To return to our illustrative light bulb: in the above scenario, I was a positive voltage ready to act upon a lower voltage. Without my creating a filament/resistor it would have been impossible to create long-lasting light (fulfillment). All that would have happened would have been the creation of a short burst of light.

Instead, though, it became another seminal moment in which I was able to see the Perfect System in action — and it changed forever the way I dealt with all potentially adverse situations. From then on, I began to use the principle of restriction with my family, my friends, and my business associates. I have never yet had cause to regret doing so.

11

The Formula

Restriction is such a powerful tool that I want to go over some of the key points that form the principle behind it. I want it to be crystal clear to you so you can use it in any given situation.

We don't like it when people try to take away the things that we perceive belong to us. Things like our self-esteem, material goods, reputation, love mates — things that make us feel fulfilled. Our reactions to incidents that are confrontational, disrespectful, and negatively charged are usually to get even, or go cold, become aloof, lash out, get physical — or just plain blow our tops.

We know from what we have learned (the laws of cause and effect) — and from our own personal experiences — that negative reactions beget negative reactions. No one wins, no one gains. When we respond in this manner, we create a negative spiral that cannot possibly produce the sustained fulfillment that we all crave. And yet, even knowing this, we still like to blow. We like it because it makes us feel good. For that split second after the first curses or the first blows are hurled, we feel great — because, right then and only right then, we feel fulfilled either because of the burst of energy or because we have defended that which makes us feel fulfilled. And we stopped them from getting it.

It doesn't last, though — it *can't* last. And there's the rub, because what we are looking for is true, lasting fulfillment. The brief imploding or exploding reaction creates an enormous sense of un-fulfillment afterwards — for the very reason that, momentarily, we were fulfilled but the feeling was snatched away.

The Perfect System tells us, with the illustration of a light bulb's filament, how it is possible to sustain constant fulfillment in our lives.

This is the process of restriction:

The very first thing for us to do in a potentially negative situation is to SHUT DOWN our reactive system. Remember: our need to react comes from our need for fulfillment, and this need always triggers a reactive impulse — SO WE MUST STOP THE REACTION. But how do we achieve this? Again, it's simple:

1. No thinking
2. No talking
3. No action

It may be for only a split second, but you must not react. The moment you shut down your reactive system, you become the cause and not the effect — thus you create an immediate affinity with the First Cause/First Creator.

Next, ask yourself the same questions mentioned earlier: "How would I like to be treated in the same situation?" and "What good will the next action I take do, not just for me but for the other person?" Is your next move going to be construc- tive or destructive for the other person?

If you go through this process, stopping the reaction and asking the questions, then the action you will take has a very good chance of being one of positive sharing. And by the laws of cause and effect, only positive sharing can come back to you from this experience. I keep reiterating this point not because I like beating dead horses but because this idea is so key to our ultimate happiness and contentment.

The moment you shut down your reactive system, you win. You may not immediately see the positive manifestation of your proactive behaviour, but it will come. It must — by the laws of the Perfect System.

Furthermore, the greatest restriction you can perform, at the moment of deciding what to do next, is to be prepared to give up everything. The great paradox here is that this is the only way to get real control and real power. The only way.

Let's discuss why this should be so.

The reasons, as usual, are straightforward: the more you give, the more you must get (for every action, there is an equal and opposite reaction), and restriction enables us, ultimately, to act like the First Cause. The more we give, the more affinity we have with the First Cause (the First Cause had everything — it was a singularity). The more affinity we have with it, the more fulfilled we feel. Elementary, no?

Restriction can become the ultimate competitive advantage in life. It enables us to move out of a reactive system — where we are merely an effect and out of control — and be in sync with the Perfect System, the proactive mindset that allows us to be the cause and, consequently, in control.

Thus, for every action that you perform, you have nobody but yourself to blame for the effect received from that action.

You also have no one else to thank. I know it's easier to blame others, but it is really your own actions alone that affect what happens to you. Remember: even when you don't see the cause and effect, they're always in play somewhere. The cause may be so distant from the effect that you discern no connection — yet there is always a connection.

I have a wonderful story to demonstrate this very principle. As described, I conduct seminars and lectures on the Perfect System. In one workshop I was giving to a class of twelve- and thirteen-year olds, a young lady challenged the notion of cause and effect. Two days before the lecture, she told me, she had had an ugly encounter on a bus after school. She, a Caucasian, was about to leave the bus from the middle door. A black male kid, who was blocking the door, looked her straight in the eye and said, "I don't like you. The next time I see your face this close to mine I'm going to bust it!"

She asked me, "Where is the cause and effect in that? I was just leaving the bus minding my own business and this kid who I hardly knew verbally assaulted me." I asked her if she was prepared to be very honest with the group and with me. She said yes. I then asked her if she was sure she had never done anything to this kid to create his reaction on the bus. She replied that he went to her school but she never had any contact with him. I kept pressing her until she had her moment of truth.

This is what she said: "Oh my God, you're right. I remember two years ago when I was in the playground talking to my girl-friends. One of them talked about 'dirty niggers' and I remember this kid standing with a group of his friends within hearing distance of this conversation and looking at me to see my response to my friend's racial slur. When I didn't say anything to my girlfriend about her foul mouth he looked at me in disgust and walked away. No wonder he thought I was the enemy! No wonder he said that stuff to me on the bus! All that anger from something that happened two years ago!"

I wasn't guessing. I knew that if she would be honest, the truth would prevail. It is our truth also. Where there's smoke, there's fire; when the sun sets, night will soon fall. The more you understand this idea, the more empowered you will become — in every situation. And the more you practise the art of restriction, the more you will come to appreciate the immense power in this concept.

~

Here are more thoughts and suggestions associated with the vital principle of restriction.

First, if you are having a tough time shutting down your reactive system, try empathizing with the other person. Try putting yourself in the other person's shoes to understand her point of view. The very fact that you have stopped everything and attempted to empathize puts you in control of both yourself and the situation. Before reacting, think about where the person lives, what kind of family life she may have, what kind of schooling she may have had, what her cultural point of view is.

Second, bear in mind that giving in to another person's demands doesn't always produce a positive effect. Acquiescing may not be the best thing for the other party or for you. Saying no can also be a way of sharing, yet for many people it is the hardest of all actions to take. Part of the human condition is that all of us, to various degrees, need to feel loved. We like to be liked. It is grounded in our need for fulfillment. We love to be loved. We need the approval of others. Thus, it becomes difficult for us to take a course of action in which we know that we'll lose someone's approval or affection.

However, by choosing the more comfortable option (saying

yes), we can frequently set in motion a long-term chain reaction of negative cause and effect. This is because the source (or the cause) is our wanting something for ourselves only, rather than seeking what is best for the other party. When this dynamic is in play, only bad stuff can happen back to you. This can be a negative spiral, and it's a big trick we continually play on ourselves. By examining the situation you are in carefully, you'll see that the problem may be that you're going against everything that you've learned about the Perfect System. This "love ambush," as I term it, can affect both your business dealings and your relationships with mates, friends, relatives, and children.

Again, it is essential to remember that this need to be loved, to be liked, is neither bad nor good. It is related to our affinity with the First Cause/First Creator. Remember that in the very beginning, all of reality was filled — totally and absolutely complete. Well, we need to connect with this state of true, long-lasting fulfillment. It is in our nature to desire this state of completeness. This is the law of affinity: like is attracted to like, matter to matter, anti-matter to anti-matter.

Following are two examples of saying no.

Your eight-year-old son wants a piece of chocolate cake, but you know that the sugar will make him hyperactive. Thus, saying no is actually best for him. But he will use every angle and gimmick he possesses to satisfy that craving. If all else fails, he will usually pull out the ultimate emotional Ninja weapon — the old dagger to the heart: "I don't love you anymore . . ." So it will always, ultimately, be easier to say yes. However, the most good that you can do for your son — rather than for yourself — is still to answer no.

A friend needs to borrow money, but she has not yet repaid money that she previously borrowed from you. Once more, the answer should be no. She may not like it — in fact she won't like it — but by saying no you give your friend the opportunity to face the irresponsible way she's been treating her friends, and you also prevent her from slipping even deeper into debt. Yet — if you can afford it, that is — it will be far easier on you to say yes. But what good would you do? What good did it do for the other person? If you did *no good* for the other person, that's what you get back — no good.

The last point to be made here is that the better you can imagine the result of an action, the better you will be able to choose the right action to take. But there is a famous adage that states, "If you can't imagine it, you can't see it." It is true, for if you can't imagine all the possibilities, you will not be able to see all their manifestations. No imagination equals no choices.

The essential lesson here is that if we don't take responsibility for our actions, we have only ourselves to blame for the consequences. Get this down pat and you will never be a victim again. In any given situation, you — and you alone — have the ability to be either a cause or an effect. The choice is yours: Leave or stay. Restrict or don't restrict. Act or react. You can never again blame anyone else for the choices you did or did not make.

12

Closure and Energy

Let's discuss genuine success in business, and to what extent the Perfect System can help us to be successful in our financial lives. After all, even though we have established that it is not money that we need, it's clear that the person who said money can't buy happiness never had any. Money is a form of transferred energy, and it is this energy — what it can do for us and others, in a very real way — that gives money its power as an abundant source of fulfillment.

Energy is a word I will be using a lot from now on.

As you have already seen, when we need to understand the fundamentals of the Perfect System we must always refer back to the beginning — the source of all physical matter. At the moment of Creation, energy was created. This energy is the universal power of the First Cause. It is the power of motion and the power of work. After Creation, this energy could not be destroyed or created; it could only be transferred and transmuted from one form to another. This energy was here before we were born and will be here after we die. It exists all around us. But in most cases it is difficult to see its true power with our limited five senses. One more thing: there is a finite amount of energy in the world and no more. In physics, this is called the closure principle.

Now, as a society, we have made coins and paper money living metaphors for energy transfer. As a result, money has the power to increase or decrease the physical quality of our lives. It is important to understand that this apparent power to alleviate our sense of lack is found not in the physical money itself but in what it can purchase or — in our terms — in what it can transform energy into: food, shelter, cars, and so on.

It should also be noted that money has no intrinsic moral value, just the potential to do good and to do bad, depending on how we decide to transform its energy value. Since it is a rule of the Perfect System that energy can be neither created nor destroyed — only transferred or transmuted — it is in the transference of this energy that we individually determine its true end value. The same ten-dollar bill can buy enough food to feed a child in Africa for a month, or it can buy enough dynamite to blow up a day care centre in Oklahoma.

I am sure that you're all familiar with the expression "I'm doing it for the money." It's absolutely true that money can buy a house, but as we've seen it's not a house that a person really wants — it's a home, a place of protection and asylum. It is this *feeling* of security, not the physical object, that gives us a sense of fulfillment.

When you buy the physical thing, its energy comes along with it. This is the only form of fulfillment that material objects bring. If you have ever rented an apartment and then bought a house, you will understand the difference of sensation. Owning has much more energy intrinsically because the property (stereos, computers, houses, etc.) becomes part of us. This occurs because we have transferred or transmuted a part of our energy into this object. We, our finite selves, are a mini microuniverse. We too have a finite amount of energy available in our finite "body" world. Let's call this amount x. When we earn money and buy material goods with a packet of our energy, we are not x plus that material thing. We are still only x. It is just that we have converted a packet of our x energy into a physical thing, which still contains the original packet of energy but is now transformed into a material possession.

This closure principle is the wisdom behind the well-known expression "There are no free lunches." We've all heard this maxim, and it's true. Nothing is for free in the universe; everything you receive for free, you have to give back as a consequence of these energy principles. If you don't earn it, you can't keep it — this is another rule of the Perfect System. Remember that each one of us has x amount of energy in our physical sphere. If we take energy into our domain that does not belong to us, we can't keep it. We must eventually lose it or get it taken away from us. We can never have more than x.

You instinctively know this to be true — and there is no place to hide from it.

Imagine that you have lunch with a friend every day for two years straight, and he always pays for the meals. How would you start to feel? Probably not very happy with the situation, right? Why? Because there is something in our nature that finds receiving all the time distasteful.

If we earn whatever it is that comes to us, we get to keep it, because we have traded energies — one thing has been exchanged for another.

This principle of the Perfect System is why thieves invariably get caught somewhere along the line: one way or another, they lose whatever they have gained illegally. Eventually, they lose the energy they received from the stolen item, and this loss will manifest itself as a physical and emotional loss equivalent to whatever it is that they stole. They may just blow the loot on high living, but lose it they will. It's a rule of the cosmos: you can't keep energy that doesn't belong to you. You can't even get to truly enjoy that energy if it was not earned. There are no free lunches, and we simply can't get away with ignoring these rules and laws. They have an impact on us one way or another. Thus, your business dealings must always be evaluated. Even if you have "beaten" somebody in a business deal and he didn't know about it, sooner or later it will have an impact on you, because you have taken what is not yours — and you know it. Your subconscious knows it, the physical laws of the universe know it. It will also affect how you feel about yourself and, consequently, how others feel about you.

We sometimes feel these laws are not personally relevant because we continually see people around us who are out-and-out crooks living to ripe old ages and dying in their sleep surrounded by their comforting families. This is an illusion. Please, never forget that we are limited by our five senses. We never know the personal hell another person is going through. Optics is not reality. It is just what appears to be. It is superficial in the sense that we are observing the surface, not the interior.

This is best demonstrated in the film *The Godfather, Part II*. Al Pacino, to all appearances, has it all: power, money, the works. Yet we see, as the story unfolds, the angst and pain he goes through as he loses his friends, his wife, and his material gains. I believe one of the reasons this movie won an Academy Award is that it resonated with real truth for all of us. I have personally known some very evil, successful people in my life. To a person, they suffered in proportion to their inequities. There is no

escape from these granite laws. Just as time separates the aware-
ness of the connection between cause and effect, optics also
creates the illusion that the laws of the Perfect System don't
have an impact on us every moment of our lives. Never assume
a truth based solely on your five senses. "Never judge a man till
you have walked in his shoes."

It is vital to be conscious of the system and its laws at all
times, especially when a new deal or venture is beginning. You
can't keep energy that you don't earn. You *can't* steal. You *can't*
take what is not yours. Make sure that the other party feels he
or she is getting, or will get, a fair deal, and that you are as concerned about his or her benefit as you are about your own.

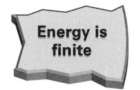

Energy is finite

13

Back to Aylmer Steinberg's Future

The way we think about ourselves is a key factor in our personal and business success.

It is a fact that most people don't have a good self-image. How many of you reading this book really like yourselves? I mean in a total way. I don't have to tell you that having low self-esteem is damaging. There is an industry built on this truth. From Leo Buscaglia to Tony Robbins, litanies have been written and spoken on this subject.

However, we are now students of the Perfect System, so we must always ask the question Why? Why is low self-esteem damaging? Because it affects the way we think and our thinking affects our actions. And we know our actions assure what will come back to us — positive or negative.

This is why we have to be so careful about how we feel about ourselves. If we have things on our minds that are not connected with success, then we will not have success — either in business or in personal relationships. If we don't "think success," we will simply not be successful.

But what is it that creates a self-image, or how we think about ourselves?

Ponder this: when we try to get energy without earning it, we create a negative loop. We cannot keep energy that we did not earn, so even if we gain in a negative way there is a deeper adverse reaction. We intuitively know that because we didn't earn whatever we've made, we cannot keep it and we will eventually have to lose it. This negative action sabotages us and does nothing to support or build a positive self-image. If we act with disregard to the laws of energy and cause and effect, we create a negative loop that makes us subconsciously undermine the success of our next opportunity. A healthy self-image occurs only when we activate our affinity with the First Cause.

No matter how long it takes, we must all finally learn that our businesses or our jobs have one real purpose: to bring us true, lasting fulfillment. It's not about making a living or making money. If we don't play by the rules, we commit ourselves to failure because we set in motion a dangerous and damaging principle: we attract, by our actions, that which we think we deserve. If we think we deserve less than everything, then that's what we will get. We are then doomed never to feel totally fulfilled. Beware, we can never really fool our true self and our elemental needs. Let me illustrate the force of this concept with a well-known story.

A wise woman who regularly sat by the roadside was approached by a traveller on horseback.

"What is the town ahead like?" inquired the traveller.

"What was the place that you just left like?" replied the wise woman.

"Frankly," confessed the traveller, "I found the townspeople to be very unfriendly and quite rude. They even cheated me in a business deal and I believe I paid too much for my room and board."

"I'm sorry to tell you but you'll find the town ahead just like the one you are coming from," said the wise woman.

The traveller rode on. An hour passed and another rider came along the road. Noticing the old woman, he asked her the same question: "What is the town ahead like?"

Again she answered, "What was the town that you just left like?"

"Why, they were a friendly lot," this traveller replied. "Quite reasonable in their business dealings and very fair in their pricing for room and board."

"Well, then," said the wise woman, "I have good news for you. The town ahead is just like the town you have come from."

The wise woman instinctively knew some of the rules of the Perfect System. She knew that we don't see things as they are, we see them as we are. A perfect example of this principle is the way the guy in my "I'm the new boss around here" story first spoke to me. In retrospect, it was obvious that he had low self-esteem, a problem so severe that he actually spoke words that he didn't intend. There can be no other plausible explanation for his actions because he was a skilled, erudite, professional businessman. This is an extreme illustration, but you get the picture.

So, in business, what you should have on your mind is not the number of customers or volume of sales or how much money you're going to make or whether the boss will be impressed with you. What you should have on your mind is what you really need: true, lasting fulfillment. The very first question you should ask yourself tomorrow morning, and every morning thereafter, is How can I gain true, lasting fulfillment?

The most powerful kind of consciousness you can inject into any business experience is one in which you truly think of others before yourself. Watch out for their interests before your own and you engage the very forces that drive the constellations themselves. Try it! People will feel exhilarated when they deal with you. They will feel so good about their experience with you that they will want to return for more — over and over again. They will also invariably tell others. To verify this, you merely have to think about it in your own experiences.

Using our knowledge of cause and effect, our understanding of the power of sharing, and the conviction of our affinity with the First Cause, we are destined for ultimate success. We cannot lose — because we have drawn ourselves into harmony with the universe around us, and the universe is never "unsuccessful." It works!

~

On a personal note, I love to go to a store that serves me respectfully and honestly — and so do you. I always pick that store over any equivalent store with similar products — and so do you. My parents did, too — and your parents as well.

As I've told you, money was scarce when I was growing up in Hamilton, but my parents always made sure we had the essentials. Whenever my brother and I needed shoes, for instance, our parents would always go to this one man who owned a shop on King Street. His name was Aylmer Steinberg, and his store was called Aylmer's Shoes. The experience of going to Aylmer's Shoes is one of the few childhood memories that have stayed with me all these years.

Going to this store was a family event. My parents had known Aylmer for a long time. I particularly remember that they trusted him. They never haggled over prices, and they never questioned his judgment. I had the sense that Aylmer knew our family and its financial situation so intimately that he would never embarrass my parents by bringing out an inappropriately pricey pair of shoes — the kind that didn't "fit" financially or culturally.

I also remember that Aylmer spent a lot of time with us as we decided on our purchases, and he was forever going back into his stock room for alternative choices. I would try on shoe after shoe, walking up and down the store, seeing how the shoes fit, until eventually my mother and father nodded their heads in approval. I was never allowed to see the actual financial transaction, of course, but I do remember that the government at that time had some sort of program that helped pay for necessities — yet I thought that my parents needed this money for more important things. Much later, I learned that Aylmer allowed his best customers to pay on a lay-away plan. Such are memories.

Today's shopping experience is a far cry from my recollections of Aylmer Steinberg, however, and I can't help but think that Aylmer, with his sales techniques, would do well in this economy, too. Walk into any large retailer's store: do you find any trace of Aylmer's Shoes? It may not be for lack of trying on the part of the retailer. In many cases, short-term bottom line realities have created a chasm between the old and the new.

Salespeople are inexperienced, under-trained in the necessary skills, or else unavailable. In the worst case, they are nonexistent. Shopping has become a chore — and this is not good for shops, let alone consumers.

What Aylmer Steinberg provided my family with would today be called one-to-one marketing, and many retailers are trying desperately to get back to it. They know that today's customers — including you and me — are tired of the lack of humanity in their purchasing experiences. They're tired of the sparse selection, the absence of "try-out time," and the lack of human focus on the part of the retailer. A whole consumer market force is demanding the return of the "Aylmer Steinberg" experience: "We want Aylmer!" — you can almost hear it. Consumers are a militant lot, too, and now they're demanding that their transactions occur when, how, and where they want them to occur. They want to be served again. And they crave the human touch. Even banks, which I consider to be retail, have electronically ATMed us to death.

We all need to feel that there is a human being responsible at the bank for our money and financial well being. We don't want a relationship with an amorphous edifice or a voice-messaging system. Why isn't there one dedicated person or team who knows my financial situation intimately? Why isn't there a familiar, responsible voice on the phone, a live human on a video screen as a personal avatar or, for important things, someone in person? Retailers who understand and acknowledge the entire spectrum of their customers' innate human needs will dominate their industries. I am not talking here about customer relationship management tools or the technology needed to deliver them. These are not the end but the means. I am speaking about what happens at the other end of the communication or transaction experience. The thing I feel when I am in your presence and when I leave it.

If you're in retail, what are you going to do? Aylmer Steinberg had the answer. Aylmer knew his business. He knew his customers' needs, and he made his customers believe that he genuinely cared for them by fulfilling those needs. Maybe he even genuinely cared for them. But whether he was a great guy or just a shrewd businessman who was totally profit-motivated, he still succeeded. He was in business for forty-four years and retired a beloved and respected member of his community. Why else do I still remember his name and his store?

Aylmer instinctively knew the how, when, where, and why of the customer experience. He was an intelligent salesperson who knew his product well, and he also knew how to match up this product with a customer's need. He gained people's trust because he always treated each customer appropriately. He was aware and respectful of their needs and of their individual financial situations. He let each customer try out products, and he offered a large selection of products to try out — the combination is unbeatable. And so it felt that to be with Aylmer Steinberg was to be nourished. You felt good about yourself, and thus you felt good about your purchase. You went in hoping and you left fulfilled, if only in that one little area of life. But at the time, that one little area is life itself.

We all have the ability to be an Aylmer Steinberg. Just follow the rules: we get back what we put in. Think back to the lesson concerning your most valued aunt, uncle, family member, or friend: it's the very same principle. Cause and effect.

It's possibly the ultimate paradox in life: the less you desire for yourself and the more you want to give others, the more you will attract others to do the same to you. I know it may seem contrary, which is why I keep driving the point home. It is a natural tendency for people to reciprocate the feelings they get from you. If they feel that you really care about them, they will really care about you. Is there really any difference between acting as if you care and genuinely caring? Like any great actor, if you act the part perfectly, you become the role — and illusion and reality are one, for all intents and purposes.

This is the same principle that makes a great brand in business. And it's what defines a good friend. Simple enough to grasp and work with, no? Obviously not, because look how many great brands — like great friendships — go down the tubes.

This is the principle upon which customer loyalty is based,

however, and it's no different from the one upon which intimate friendship is based. I didn't invent this: I'm just observing it, and it is all around us, for those of us with eyes to see.

The most successful corporations are the ones that have identified sharing as a quintessential aspect of their operation. It's in their mission statement, and they deliver on that statement all the way through, from the way they treat their employees to the way they treat their customers. Take the Walt Disney Co. and Starbucks Coffee. Here are enterprises where this concept is more than just a matter of lip service: it's a consciousness infusing their whole existence, a genuine commitment to a universal principle. And the reward is astonishing success.

Also, such companies never limit their imaginative sweep: there's no theoretical end to how much they can give back — and thus there's no end to their growth. Growth results from what is returned to them — in other words, corporate fulfillment. And this, in turn, is handed to — and passed back from — shareholders, who also seek fulfillment. As businesspeople, we should never forget this: what is good for the goose is good for the gander — and all the other geese.

What everybody wants — no exceptions — is true, lasting fulfillment. This must become the uppermost thought in your mind. Never limit how much fulfillment you are capable of receiving. Otherwise you are limiting not only how much fulfillment you can receive but also what others can gain through you.

There is a story about two fishermen who are fishing beside each other. One man notices that the guy next to him keeps catching big fish and throwing them back in, yet when he catches a small fish he keeps it. So the first man says, "What's the matter? Don't you like the taste of big fish?"

The other fisherman replies, "Oh no, I love big fish, but they won't fit into my frying pan."

Here is the deal: I'm not talking about your getting a bigger frying pan. I'm talking about you having a pan of limitless size. Can you conceive of this?

Why limit yourself and your imagination? You are only curtailing your unlimited possibilities. Yet if you think it can't be done, you're damn right: it can't.

Keep thinking "Aylmer Steinberg."

I do.

14

Validation and the
Merchants of Guilt

As Aylmer's story proves, giving what you need to someone else first entitles you to get that very thing back. By performing a physical action for someone else's good, you can actualize the fulfillment of your own need and yourself. You can make it so. You can create a new reality that is validated because it is observable. Before, what you wanted (fulfillment) and who you were (cause) existed only in potential. If potential is not converted into actuality, it has no power, because, by definition, it is not real.

Actions (not words or thoughts) are the only true expression we accept in formulating our opinions and judgments of others. This is because we are, by nature, social animals that interact. This interaction is governed by the approval and validation of others. Actions are the amino acids of relationships. They are the building blocks that allow us to judge others with respect to permission, expectations, and intimacy. Actions tell others who we are. They are also the driving force of what psychology calls our self-image. Self-image is defined as the kind of person we think we are, our character and personality. Having an accurate self-image is an essential element in our quest for personal fulfillment.

It is important to note that an accurate self-image can only exist when there is no conflict in the way I see myself and the way others see me.

This self-image thing is a tricky business. How do you see yourself? Are you adventurous or shy, caring or bullying? Are you generous or thrifty? The descriptions are as numerous as the myriad of human personality traits. Why is it that we need others to verify and validate how we feel about ourselves? Because we are adventurous or shy, kind or hurtful only if someone else thinks we are. I may think that I am a kind and sensitive person, but if those around me think the opposite, I obviously have a very serious problem.

That problem creates a critical construct called an inaccurate self-image: if we are not in sync with how others perceive us, then there is a good chance that we will see as unwarranted and unfair the way those people respond to and treat us. It is like being in a fun-house hall of mirrors — we never get to see ourselves the way we think we are. We are always distorted in some fashion when we are with others who don't see us as we see ourselves. If this happens for a long enough time, our reality becomes distorted like the mirror and we become stressed, insecure, and dislocated from our physical environment.

As stated, actions are critical to the possession of an accurate self-image. If you see yourself as a generous person but never convert that generosity into action, then, according to the Perfect System's laws and rules, you are not generous. To be generous means to perform acts of generosity. This might seem obvious, yet apply it to some of the epithets you reserve for yourself — wise, good-natured, loving, hard-working — and see how many hold up to scrutiny. "By your deeds they shall know you." In this world we are judged and acknowledged by our fellow human beings solely through our actions.

And the business lesson to be learned here is profound. All we have to do is replace the words *I* or *you* with the word *brand*. A brand is like a person. It has personality, which generates expectations, permission, and intimacy, just as we do.

But a brand loses effectiveness when it no longer has an accurate self-image — in other words, when what a company thinks about its products or services differs from what the consumer thinks. At this point, it is futile for a company to advertise because the advertising only exacerbates the situation. All the marketing in the world will not change the way the consumer thinks about the company's products or services. The company keeps telling consumers the same thing but, no matter how sophisticated, intelligent, and costly the manner of communication is, the consumer believes the message isn't true.

Remember, I can have a healthy self-image only when I see myself as others see me. And the only way I can actualize that self-image is by actions — not simply by words or thoughts.

Think of all the marketing damage control that Exxon engaged in after the *Valdez* oil spill: "We care about nature." Did anyone buy it? I know I didn't. This is a precise example of inaccurate self-imaging. Most corporations and associations are plagued with this disease, and it results in the waste of valuable below-the-line, after-tax marketing dollars. Because many corporate leaders are unaware of the self-defeating spiral they are creating, they feel an enormous sense of frustration that can be felt throughout their whole organizations. Their advertising and marketing create systemic corporate angst and disenfranchised customers.

Having an accurate self-image is a critical factor in creating a successful business, yet many companies in North America continue to suffer in ignorance of this principle, becoming neurotic in the process. They act neurotically when, for example, they begin to think that the competition is the enemy, or that we as customers have to be manipulated or bamboozled in order to find their product attractive. This state of mind, however, only generates the eventual loss of top-level employees and leads to slumping sales. I have seen such corporate paranoia many times in my career. It's always a shame to see it happening, too, because it doesn't have to be so. With the application of the above principles, any company would be able to turn itself — and its self-image — around in very little time. The Perfect System, I'll remind you yet again, is universal — it works for people, corporations, boards of directors, stars, planets, trees, and rocks.

I would like to discuss here a nuance of accurate self-imaging that I feel is almost as important as what we've been discussing.

What happens when we perform an act of generosity that is misperceived as an act of selfishness? I give to a charity, say, but some people view my giving as self-serving because they think I gave so that others would think me generous, or that I gave because I wanted the kudos and attention it brought to me and to my organization.

"In life," as Yogi Berra put it, "perception is nine-tenths of the law." No matter what I do, there will always be some people who distort the reasons behind my actions. But this is not a problem of having an inaccurate self-image — it is a problem of other people's jealousy and greed distorting my real motivation. This is usually fuelled by their lack of fulfillment. Not to forget that we all need to feel fulfilled — friends, family, customers, co-workers. Feeling fulfilled is an equal-opportunity need.

However, be aware of people who create a warped mirror that inaccurately reflects your real truth. When you see yourself through their malevolent eyes, what you are seeing is not the real you. It is just their distorted view.

Thus, it is essential to surround yourself with people who are accurate mirrors, true reflections of who you are. These are the people you can trust to reflect accurately because they truly care for you and for your well-being. They are the only mirrors you should use when verifying your true self-image. Start discerning who around you are your "accurate" mirrors and who are your "inaccurate" mirrors. People who are critical are not necessarily "inaccurate" mirrors. Criticism is not your judge of accuracy. Intent is.

As I have noted, we are surrounded in this world by people who are unfulfilled, who are in a constant state of deprivation. Many of them attempt to correct this state of being with quick fixes like drugs, alcohol, crime, violence, abuse, egotism, and all the other plagues that human flesh is heir to. This is not a judgment but a fact. And this fact now leads us to the important question What exactly is our responsibility to others?

Please, please remember this: we are responsible to others, not *for* others. The only person we are responsible *for* is ourselves. Are we responsible *to* others? Absolutely. I am responsible for providing financial, emotional, and physical support to those I care for. But I am not responsible *for* them. Each one of us must take total responsibility for our own lives.

People who think they are responsible *for* other people's lives are usually control freaks and energy vampires; they are the twenty-first century's slavers. They are dangerous and must be treated as such. Those who feel responsible for others create disastrous relationships with their co-workers, children, mates, and parents. They want us to be eternal children so they can take care of us — and, in doing so, of course, never allow us our sacred right to take responsibility for our own lives.

Then there are those who want us to be responsible *for* them. This latter group is just as dangerous as the first group of emotional thugs, but much more difficult to identify. They're masters of control, because their offering confuses us. They are the professional victims — those who don't want to take responsibility for their own lives. They want us to be responsible *for* them. They are the merchants of guilt. Here's an analogy I think will show you the power they wield.

There is a mystical Islamic sect known as the Whirling Dervishes, who achieve a state of spiritual ecstasy by going to an isolated part of the desert at night and dancing around a fire. With their colourful robes streaming through the air, they whirl faster and faster as they dance. So hypnotic is their motion that onlookers sitting by the campfire become entranced and soon cannot help but join in — it is the only way they have of making a spiritual connection of their own.

Now, the negative people around us use this same principle intuitively, but for nonspiritual ends. They twirl and dance crying, "Poor me," "None of this is my fault," "You don't love me anymore," and "Life dealt me a lousy hand." They chant and they whirl, and we seem to get caught up in the mesmerizing ceremony. Suddenly, we too are dancing and spinning and saying things like, "Let me take care of that for you," "You poor thing," and "Let me give you something because I feel so guilty about your circumstances." Do you recognize the experience?

We would do these dancers less harm by saying, "Sorry, I'm not dancing!" "No, I will not take responsibility for your life!" It is okay for you to respond like this, because now you understand that you can't give somebody something if he or she doesn't earn it or doesn't really want it. Complaining is not earning. It's a song-and-dance routine. You can give these people what they want, of course, but why would you do that when they can't keep it? Why would you do that when you will also have prevented them from using the opportunity to learn a prime rule of the Perfect System? This is another case of learning when not to give in, when not to say yes.

We are all responsible for the consequences of our own actions, and we *do* have a responsibility to others. But if those professional victims wish to be depressed or negative, then so be it. That is their responsibility. The distance between *to* and *for* is wider than the Grand Canyon.

There is one exception to the above rule and that has to do with young children. As I stated before, we are totally responsible to and for their well-being, intellectually, spiritually, and physically. We are their guardians until they reach an age where they are conscious of cause and effect. Any neglect of this duty puts them in absolute harm's way.

Now, armed with these truths, we should never again have to buy into the negative vortices of guilt merchants and energy vampires. For, you see, if we stop feeding them with our precious energy, they will eventually have to face the truth themselves. If you truly care for such people, be humane and stop their pain.

It will be difficult at first to identify the difference between being responsible *to* and *for*. But it won't be impossible — so give it time. For if we are to get back into control of our lives, we must never again deal in negative currency. Guilt is the gold standard of negative currency — the guilt-edged stock. Don't deal in it, don't even barter in it. You will never be in control as long as others control you.

Perform your actions because you want to be like the First Cause, not because you feel guilty. There is nothing for you in guilt.

One more thing on this same theme. Now that you are beginning to understand and, I hope, are starting to use the Perfect System, you can never play the role of teacher when there is no student. There can be no coercion in the Perfect System. Do not pour water where there is no container to hold it — you will be transferring energy to a place where there is no vessel to receive it. Your action will be wasted — and wasting energy is a big no-no in the Perfect System. As physics tells us, the sum of the energy in the universe is conserved. There is only so much to go around (the closure principle). We must cherish and treasure all the energy in our domain — because every domain has its energy limit. We are given x amount of energy to use in our lives, and how we convert that energy is our individual responsibility. It is your obligation to share this information with others, just as I have with you. Always remembering the valuable lesson of the difference between *to* and *for*.

This is a good time for you to jot down the kinds of situations and relationships that are in the *to* and *for* paradigm. Always be honest in your assessments. Now think about the actions that would do the most good for the people on your list.

15

Thesis, Antithesis, Synthesis, and the Digital Revolution

In my opinion, the lessons of the Perfect System are becoming even more relevant in the new business era. In the new economy, business, by necessity of the market's expectations, must be a blend of both bricks and mortar and digital enterprise. An organization cannot compete and ultimately survive in the new millennium otherwise.

Digital convergence saves money, creates more efficient supply chains, and allows for customer interaction at the most profound one-to-one level. There are lots of books for you to read if you want to know about e-commerce and technology trends; just go to my website at www.theperfectsystem.com and you will get a list of my recommendations. However, few people are talking about the why of this digital revolution. Why is it growing so fast, and why is it changing the face of business as we know it? The answer lies at the centre of the Perfect System, in the innate power of networks. But I am jumping ahead of myself. Let's begin at the beginning and look at the science of analogue and digital technology.

Analogue communication is physical and, in many cases, is based upon the movement of physical particles — for example, in a videotape or an audio cassette. Information is recorded and played by the magnetizing of ferrous oxide particles. This process gets these particles positioned and moving in specific directions. Digital communication, however, moves in a non-physical manner. It reduces its mechanics to a code of two digits — zeroes and ones. Unlike physical particles, these zeroes and ones have a unique connection with each other. They create what is called a binary relationship. They are absolute opposites. Zero is nothing; one is something. Zeroes and ones in this configuration create an innate natural tension. Sound familiar? The new frontier of the virtual, digital world is based upon the two elemental realities of our universe that live together in the same compromising harmony — determinism and indeterminacy (Newtonian and quantum mechanics). In principle,

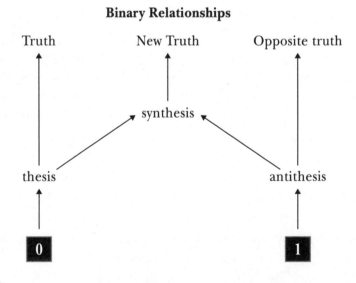

Binary Relationships

whenever you have opposites you also have what the nineteenth-century German philosopher Georg Wilhelm Friedrich Hegel called a dialectic. Hegel puts it well. He says that when you have two ideas in opposition, they can also be thought of as a thesis and an antithesis. And when this occurs, something odd happens: the stage is set for an eventual new creation, a third entity called a synthesis — a new idea or thought arising from the combined intelligence and energy of the two opposites. He calls it the "union of union and non-union." Some examples of this principle are war versus peace = cold war; rich versus poor = bourgeoisie; photograph (life frozen on film) versus life (live, moving people) = motion pictures; and the ever popular yes versus no = maybe.

In these examples lies the intrinsic power of our universe and of digital communication. One idea and its complete opposite have the intrinsic possibility that forces an entirely new idea. In its most elemental form, this process creates a network. Note that physical or digital networks have no intrinsic morality. Like everything in the Perfect System, they are neither good nor bad. They just are. We create the value in our business, in our relationships, in our ideas, and in our networks. The Internet, for example, has everything from pornography to "The Sermon on the Mount." I wouldn't want it any other way. You see, the Perfect System enables me to create my own personal value by making me responsible for what I do and allowing me to connect with my affinity with the First Cause. That way I can keep what I earn.

If a person wishes to do business in the e-commerce market he must have others who champion and buy into his ideas. In the old analogue business model, it was possible to do it yourself — much as I was able to create an entire jingle business solely with my own talents. In the new digital model, on-line business execution issues are much more complex, so that one person cannot know enough, or possess sufficient skills necessary, for the execution of any commercial idea. We will all thus need to create partnerships, consortiums, and groups of believers.

Digital networks, unlike most of their analogue predecessors, have a psychological basis as well as an economic one. What exactly is that psychology? The World Wide Web gives us the answer: utter, unabashed sharing. The Internet is so shamelessly successful because it taps directly into the truths of the Perfect System. Partners, consortium members, or believers will play with you only if you act in a balanced way. They may play for a while — as long as it suits them — but if they don't think you are sharing to the extent that you should be sharing, they won't stay in the game for the long run. And the long run is the only place where you really want to play in this brave new world.

The opportunities here are stunningly unparalleled. Where it used to take twenty years, if not more, to build a brand, doing so today, courtesy of the inherent power of digital networks, happens so fast that the process would have been dismissed as science fiction even ten years ago. I call it Hydroponic Branding, for, like a plant in artificial light and soil, this new branding doesn't need the old model of sun, earth, and water to grow at a steady, predictable pace. Look at what Amazon.com, MP3, and Autobytel.com have accomplished in such a short time. WinZip, File Ferret, and Norton went from nothing and nowhere to become princes of the market in less time than it took Time Inc. to construct its corporate headquarters fifty years ago. Remember: the rules and laws of the Perfect System are universal. They are valid in real *and* in virtual worlds.

Things are moving so fast in this virtual space that by the

time this book is published, there will not only be scores of other successful examples but it is possible that the examples I have used may have become passé and irrelevant as other hydroponic brands win the coveted battle for consumers' eyeballs and hearts.

16

Brands and the Perfect System

I believe that brand is more than simply advertising and marketing. A brand must be in the air that you breathe when you come into the environment or presence of an organization. It is the oxygen that employees, suppliers, and, most important, your customers breathe.

Indeed, if the will is there, an organization can control the effect and composition of that oxygen so that it can predict and control how those different constituents feel and respond to that organization. Whether one feels elated and nourished or blasé and unmoved is controllable in any enterprise environment. This is as true for a bricks-and-mortar business as it is for a corporate website. However, it is critical to understand that behaviour is the essential element in this corporate oxygen. I call this concept and its methodology Systemic Branding. As I have discussed, only an action can truly validate or change an opinion. Advertising and marketing serve only to inform your constituents about what you are "doing." What you are doing isn't simply in the words (advertising, marketing, and speeches) but is also in the physical action of change. This knowledge about behaviour and its impact will keep employees from moving, keep customers from buying somewhere else, and keep suppliers continually supporting your success.

Behaviour becomes one of the essential elements to success in this new economy of blended business (virtual and physical). It is such a powerful force because it is rooted in our elemental need for fulfillment. Here's the issue: if I am looking to buy a product and the price, delivery time, and quality are basically equivalent among competitors, why would I choose to shop in your corporate environment (physical and virtual) rather than your competitor's environment? The answer is as true for me as it is true for you. We will go where we feel the most nourished. I will always return to an environment where someone is dedicated to making me feel fulfilled. I do it in my friendships, I do it with my business relationships, and I do it when I shop.

This is not rocket science. Proper behaviour creates nourishment, nourishment creates trust, and trust creates Permission. I have capitalized the word because I believe that Permission will become one of the prime corporate assets of the new economy: it deserves recognition. When you have Permission, you have the right to fail and the right to succeed. Here's an anecdote that illustrates in a small way the power of Permission and the intricacies involved in it.

I was hired about seven years ago by the Canadian Broadcasting Corporation to help them with an audience numbers problem. It seemed that their internal research was giving a different reading on the amount of time the average Canadian spent watching CBC programming compared to what the Nielsen ratings were indicating. This was a matter of concern because advertising revenue is predicated on these Nielsen numbers. In this case, the Nielsen numbers were some four points lower than the CBC's numbers. My job was to help solve this discrepancy, but off the top I wanted to see if I could discover why this difference had occurred in the first place. I did — and it was startling. It appeared that the CBC and Nielsen numbers were both correct.

How was this possible? The answer had to do with Permission. The Nielsen numbers at that time were defined by a randomly selected group of viewers who would, basically, check off on a piece of paper the shows they had watched that day. The problem was that these "average" viewers were embarrassed to admit they watched the CBC. The CBC had never had the glamour of other networks and so the Nielsen responders bent the truth. Many denied watching shows that they had actually viewed.

When I discovered that the issue was essentially one of brand permission, the solution was self-evident. I would have to make it permissible for people to publicly admit they watched the CBC. So I created a campaign called "Go Public," enlisting the help of famous Canadians like Joe Flaherty from Second City, Leonard Cohen the poet and musician, Timothy Findley the novelist, and Moses Znaimer, president of a competing TV station. There were ten such luminaries in all, and I filmed each one in an interview setting in which they all spoke in a candid manner about what the CBC meant to them. Then I cut each interview into a thirty-second commercial. The commercials were honest, powerful, and real. In a very personal way, each interviewee acknowledged that not only was the CBC a truly valuable part of Canadian broadcasting history but also it had an important and continuing influence on each one of their lives.

The TV campaign was aired, and the next Nielsen ratings

accurately reflected what the CBC had suspected all along: the viewership ratings increased by the lost four points. My group of third-party endorsers made it permissible for viewers to say they watched the CBC.

It was all about Permission.

In 1985, when Coke decided to launch the new Coke, they quickly realized that they had breached their customers' trust. Within weeks, the consistent message that came back from Coke drinkers was, "Coke is not your brand, it's *our* brand — keep your hands off it!" Coke clearly did not have permission from its constituents to change the Coke formula. The company quickly responded with the launch of Coke Classic. Coke's arrogant presumption of its customers could have killed a lesser brand. Illustrating once again that Permission must never be underestimated.

~

I would now like to return to the theme of proper behaviour. Let me pose this question: How many corporations do you know that think about behaviour and the way it affects their employees, suppliers, and customers? In my experience, I would say the answer is only a handful. But they do exist. I have already mentioned Starbucks and the Walt Disney Co. However, the organization that comes closest to understanding intuitively the power of Systemic Branding is, from my personal business experience, the McDonald's Corporation. Here is a company that created a product catering to the level of satisfaction that families need — a safe, clean environment that delivers consistently well-prepared, reasonably priced fast food. They do this better than any of their competitors. But they also consistently deliver something else, an intangible product that I believe supersedes their physical offering.

I will illustrate this intangible product by sharing an experience that I had about ten years ago. I had just finished working thirty-six hours straight finishing a campaign for a client. I had been recording in the studio for all that time, so I needed to get out, catch some fresh air, grab a bite to eat. There was a McDonald's in a mall near the studio, so I hopped in my car and drove there. It was three o'clock in the afternoon, and I was the only customer in the store. Behind the counter was this lovely blue-haired older woman. I looked at her, she looked at me, and as our eyes met she started to sing in a strong, confident voice, "You deserve a break today." It was McDonald's jingle at the time, but for me, it couldn't have been more appropriate, because that is *exactly* what I needed — and she recognized and acknowledged it. What a lesson! I learned more that day about effective marketing than any other single experience in my business life has taught me. This is what I saw:

An employee bought in to the promise of her company's external marketing message so much that she was prepared to deliver it on the floor, on the job. This wasn't about marketing anymore. She was controlling the air I was breathing in that McDonald's. She *nourished* me. And I gave that nourishment back by telling her how much I appreciated her kindness and sensitivity . . . and I bought lots of food, more than I wanted, because it was my pleasure. This is the same organization that created Ronald McDonald House (a place where parents of sick kids in hospitals can stay), in-store protected playgrounds, and Happy Meals. They were taking, but they were also giving back, and we rewarded them in return. We rewarded them by making McDonald's the largest fast-food chain in the world. We rewarded them by buying their corporate stock. We rewarded them by allowing them to make mistakes and not taking away our business when these errors of judgment occurred. They dropped the ball big time on their Adult Meals, but it was just a little bump in the flow. Other companies' stocks would have plummeted. Not McDonald's.

However, the most powerful example of their good will, their sheer Permission, is when the story broke a couple of years ago about a woman who burned herself while opening a steaming hot McDonald's coffee. Ultimately, no one gave a damn. In fact, we sided with McDonald's and thought her lawsuit greedy and frivolous. Such is the power of Systemic Branding. Its effect is so profound because it encompasses many of the rules of the Perfect System.

17

No Pain, No Gain

What is it that limits our ability to be successful? Even when we have the information, why is it always so difficult to remember what it is that we have learned and to put it into practice every day of our lives? Why do we always fall back to our old reactive selves? What's going on? Are we stupid or something?

This may alarm some of you, but we all have an enemy that does not want us to succeed, an enemy that, if left to its own devices, will sabotage us at every opportunity. Who on earth is this person? You may well ask!

I'm sorry to report that it is me. It is you. It is us. I'm talking about our physical bodies. Here is another important rule of the Perfect System: physical objects have an innate desire for self-preservation and for the conservation of their own energies.

The body — yours and mine — is just another physical object. Our hearts beat without being told to and cease to beat against our will. If we get a sore or cut, our white corpuscles start to assault the infection without our consciously telling them to. The body is programmed to survive. That's the message carried in our DNA: keep on keeping on!

Take two people on a raft who have just survived a shipwreck. No food, no water — you've seen the movie. The will to survive is incredibly powerful. It's part of our bodies' very nature. But this desire to survive is for itself alone. The great truths of the universe, however, tell us that only by sharing, by implementing and acting on our affinity with the First Cause, can we truly feel content, can we truly be in control of our lives. Does this sound like a conflict of interest?

Yes, my friends, I'm sorry to report that we actually are our own worst enemies. We stop ourselves from being happy. But again, this is neither good nor bad. It is merely the human condition. We must simply be ever mindful of this innate conflict. We must shoulder the burden of it and always bear it in mind. The good news is that the body also contains a mind, a mind that has the ability to be rational, to be intuitive, and to exercise free will. Human intelligence has the innate ability to balance our need for protection and survival with our need for long-lasting fulfillment. The mind is the perfect metaphor for our micro-universe of determinism and indeterminacy. It is physical and predictive, creative and unpredictable. We must learn to keep both in balance and in harmony — just as the macro-universe does.

What else limits our ability to be successful? Life, by its very nature, is full of tests. And because we are all part of the physical world, we cannot avoid these challenges. We must begin to see them as opportunities to grow, to learn, to understand how things work. As you read the following tale, think about the rule that we must earn what we wish to keep.

Once upon a time, in a field, a man found the cocoon of a

butterfly and took it home. One day, a small opening appeared in the cocoon, and the beautiful insect that it contained was slowly born. The man sat in wonderment and watched this butterfly for several hours as it struggled to force its body through the little hole. Eventually, it seemed to cease making any more progress, as if it had got as far as possible and could go no further. The man decided to help the butterfly. He took a pair of scissors and snipped away at the remaining bits of cocoon, until finally the butterfly emerged easily. However, it had a swollen body and very small wings. So the man continued to watch it closely, because he expected, at any moment, to see the wings enlarge in order to support the obese body, which he imagined would in time contract.

But this did not happen. In fact, the butterfly spent the rest of its brief life crawling around in the dirt with a swollen body and shrivelled wings. It never was able to fly.

What the man, in his kindness and haste, did not understand was that the restricting cocoon, and the struggle required for the butterfly to get through its tiny opening, was a way of forcing fluid from the butterfly's body into its wings so that, once free of the cocoon, it would be ready for flight.

Thus it follows that, sometimes, hardship, pain, or struggles are exactly what we need in our lives. A baby or child protected from all the common childhood diseases will not develop an immune system to protect it from more serious infections. It is a well-known fact that business is defined as a closed system (a limited mass with uncrossable boundaries, like a watch). Business experts say that the only way to expand a closed system, as in the case of a business that is not growing, is to infect it with a virus or chaos. The system then will either die or grow healthier in response.

If we were allowed to go through life without any obstacles, it could possibly cripple us. At the very least, we wouldn't be as strong as we could have been. And we could certainly never fly!

The Perfect System shows us that where there is pain or struggle there is also unequalled opportunity for growth. Often, we can't see this opportunity, either because the pain is so severe or because it caught us off guard. Sometimes, we hate the pain because we don't think we deserve it. Nonetheless, whatever else it may do, physical pain tells us that something is wrong. If the pain continues, we visit a doctor for advice and healing.

It should be noted that some physical pain can have an emotional root. I know that when I am stressed or angry or disappointed with myself, I tend to get a tightening in the chest. I sweat profusely too, and usually I get a headache. Yet when you come to understand the laws that govern the universe, you begin to see that pain, intrinsically, is neither good nor bad. It is valueless. It is what we do with the pain that gives it its value. I am a perfect example of the value of pain. I had absolutely no pain with my stenosis of the spine. Had I felt pain I could have had the operation sooner and saved many of my now atrophied muscles. After that incident, I stopped complaining about any pain that I was feeling, realizing that it was simply an alarm going off to indicate that I had a physical problem that needed looking after or that I was potentially in a growth situation.

Try it! The next time you get an ordinary headache (migraines don't count in this example) or a backache, think about the principle involved here. You could have the pain because you have some kind of inner struggle. The struggle could be with a thought, or a person, or an action you have performed, or with something that someone has done to you. Think about where the opportunity for growth is waiting in your pain. Could you have controlled a situation better? Could you have done something in a different way, a way that was more sharing? Could you have created more fulfillment?

Think of the light bulb. Are you creating the maximum light or are you short-circuiting? Whatever answer you get, you have just started a process of converting pain and struggle into growth, control, and personal healing.

18

Fear, Sadness, and Other Challenges

What is fear? What are the things in life that make us afraid? Look:

- Fear is despair in the face of the unknown.
- Fear is the result of an anticipation of danger or pain.
- We feel fear when we don't trust in the certainty of cause and effect.
- We feel fear when we live in the world of the five senses.
- We feel fear when we see only the fragmentation of reality and not the big picture.

In my observations, human fear is directly related to the principles of physical matter and its basic innate requirement for survival. As I explained in the previous chapter, in the physical world self-preservation is a primal force. Trees don't fly off into space, matter will not change form unless acted upon, and humans will generally take every possible action to avoid death.

In the physical world, we are fearful of anything that threatens our perceived state of physical well-being or threatens anything that we believe belongs in our physical domain (family, money, employment, reputation, etc.). Remember that we need to feel fulfilled because of our affinity with the First Creator/First Cause. Understandably, we are threatened by and fearful of anything that will make us feel less fulfilled.

However, fear is positive when the threat is real. In some instances, it is prudent and advisable to be fearful. When we are in a truly life-threatening situation, our senses alert us to the danger. Crossing the street, we hear a car screeching to a halt. Our senses tell us we are in danger, and we then begin to react to avoid the threat either by stopping and gathering more information or by quickly moving away from the threat. Our adrenaline is pumping and our body is in a full stress alert; but we have avoided physical loss. Someone attacks our reputation, and because it is a physical part of who we are, we go into the same fearful mode. An investment opportunity comes up, but we are afraid of losing money because money represents the energy of physical protection and well-being for us and our family.

Now that we understand the source of fear (physical loss), we can now observe this phenomenon from an intellectual distance. This will allow us to distinguish a real threat from an illusory threat. Why put ourselves through a "full body press" when there really is no danger of loss? In the case of the investment opportunity, once we understand the source of the fear that we are feeling we will be able to look at the risks and rewards of the investment separate from the irrational impairment of that fear. In fact, it is reasonable for us to be fearful of financial loss. But the investment may not be all that risky, and the upside is that we will create more financial wealth for ourselves and our family and indeed feel more fulfilled. The key to clear decision-making comes from understanding where the fear response comes from. The more we see the big picture, the better the choices and opportunities for personal fulfillment. Use fear. Don't let it use you.

Now we come to sadness. Does the Perfect System have a solution for sadness? Absolutely!

We always feel negative emotions when we are not fulfilled. We can feel angry, resentful, threatened. But sadness is directly connected to the feeling of being a victim. Our boss or neighbour or spouse or God or the universe — someone — is not treating us fairly, not giving us what we deserve. We believe that we deserve more than we are getting. What we are getting, we think, is the short end of the stick. But looking outside ourselves for the culprit who is creating this lack of fulfillment is just reactive behaviour — the kind that creates veils between us and the truth. The effect of such behaviour is merely to draw more sadness into our lives.

What is the first step to take to stop the feelings of despair and sadness? The first step is to acknowledge that you alone are responsible for your personal sense of fulfillment. And you alone are responsible for your feelings of despair and sadness for this lack. Someone or something else didn't do this to you — you did it to yourself. Be honest with yourself and then get on with the remedy.

The act of sharing is a sure-fire solution for sadness. Come out of yourself for a moment. Start closing the gap between you and the First Cause. Do what the First Cause would do. Start giving without consideration for your own needs. Give to others so that they may receive what it is that you are craving. You must start the process in order to ultimately receive what you desire. Don't be afraid; the system *is* perfect. You will not fail — you cannot fail.

Let me repeat yet again: every time we perform an action, we draw energy. If what we do is positive, we draw positive energy for ourselves. If what we do is negative, we draw negative energy to ourselves. Again we see Newton's third law of motion at play — for every action there is an equal and opposite reaction. Negative energy creates a veil over us that separates us from reality, that pulls us apart from our real consciousness, that distances us from our true affinity, that creates an abyss between us and our real truth.

Imagine a long line of dominoes:

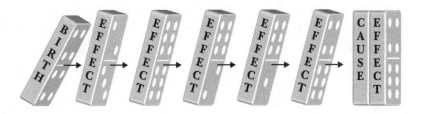

Now imagine that the first domino is your first moment of consciousness as a child. Follow down the line of dominoes until you reach the last one, which is where you are now. This illustrates the point I made earlier that, all your life, you have been a series of effects. You are joined inextricably to their line of consequences — what I call the Effect Line. Any emotional pain that you are feeling right now is undoubtedly real. Some of you have been abused as children, physically or emotionally; some have had great personal loss, material or non-material; and some of you have felt hurt during the growing process itself. You are all attached to this line of events. They have formed you emotionally and socially — perhaps even physically.

They are the things that happened to you, the things that make you who you are, much in the same way that I was a self-protecting, self-interested, self-absorbed egocentric when I first met my future wife. We've all been in the same boat, so there's no need for shame or pride.

But why is it so difficult for us to change, to break this negative cycle? Why can't we easily convert the next possible effect into a cause?

The first reason is somewhat obvious: there is great comfort in the familiarity of who we are and how we react to things. The moment that we transform an effect into a cause we separate ourselves from the events that formed us — and that's pretty scary stuff! It's "what we know." When we separate ourselves from the effect, it can appear that we also risk losing ourselves, losing the person we know.

If we really want to change, though, we *must* separate ourselves from the Effect Line. We must objectify it, look at it from a distance, use it as a reference point. What you're telling yourself should be "See that Effect Line over there? That's what made me the kind of person I am today. However, I'm now separate from it. I respect it because it existed and was true and it made me the person I am today. But I have the ability to change that truth because I have free will and I choose to change."

Always remember there exists in this physical world a balance between determinism and free will. Nothing is written unless you say it is written. Yes, there is cause and effect, but there is also our ability to change our destiny. This understanding is humankind's greatest power.

It is what separates us from the rest of the physical kingdom.

Use this free will to be the agent of change in your life. It is yours to have because it is part of your affinity with the First Cause.

It is your escape tool out of the "prison with no bars." Sadly, as long as you are prepared to be an effect, you will never have control over what happens next in your life.

This, my friends, is the ultimate life sentence. The first step out of this incarceration is simple in nature, yet fundamentally most difficult because we need to go against our nature.

~

Here's a scenario for potential first-steppers. Tomorrow morning when you wake up, you are going to start feeling things. These things are attached to the line of effect dominoes, beginning with your first conscious moment. Try for a split second to restrict; be like the filament in the light bulb. Push back and try to separate yourself from your feelings and try not to feel anything for that moment. Shut down your reactive mind: no thoughts, no words, no actions.

It is in this moment that you have taken an action of restriction and, in doing so, have at last become a cause. Be vigilant: your past is going to try drawing you back into the Effect Line with its experiences. These are very powerful, very comforting, and they're what you know. But keep at it, particularly during a day when you experience negative feelings. Just focus on shutting down the reactive system. You'll keep getting drawn back into the Effect Line, of course, but that's okay. You're working. You're sawing through those invisible prison bars. Keep restricting whenever you get the strength to separate yourself from those negative experiences. Easy and slow is the way — slow and steady. This is how you build up your new line of experiences: the experiences of being a cause.

When I became sick with diabetes and stenosis of the spine, I had times of severe depression brought on by a combination of my sugar levels (chemical) and the fact that all I had built was falling apart in front of my eyes (emotional). Once I got my diabetes under control, I had to deal with the terrible lows that were purely emotional. What saved me was an opportunity that arose with a close business friend. He had a multimedia division of his advertising agency that was doing poorly. He had lost $250,000 in the previous year and asked if I would help him. He told me that he couldn't pay me because he was just coming out of a tough financial period. He thought that a couple of days a week of my time would suffice to fix his problem.

The last thing I wanted to do was leave the house and schlep downtown. My walking was unsteady, I felt terrible, and I was entirely self-absorbed. But I knew the rules of the Perfect System and I made (to me) the Herculean effort to help my friend out. That action was my first step into emotional well-being. In essence, I broke the Effect Line. Each day became a little easier until I was feeling good about myself all the time. I was acting like a cause and I was back in control.

This method works for most people. It worked for me — but it won't work for you unless you try it. There are, however, some people in such deep depressions that they can't even take this first step. There is no way for them to sever their relationships with their feelings. They are so far into their negative spirals that they don't have the physical stamina and emotional strength to pull themselves out of their tailspins.

Are these people lost forever in this uncontrolled horror? Are they doomed to the eternal intake of antidepressant drugs and therapy? Are they the damned?

They are damn well not, fortunately — and we should never dismiss people thus. The Perfect System has allowed for a half step that can be taken before initiating the first step. It is not predicated on breaking free of the emotional hold of the Effect Line. All people need do is perform a simple act of giving, an action for someone besides themselves. When you perform an act of giving, you reconnect to your affinity with the First Cause. When you are in the "affinity" mode, you begin to disentangle the hold that your "effect" emotions have on you. Remember: the First Cause was an explosion, not an implosion. It was an act of out-giving.

We are attached to that First Cause and by acting like it, we become more like it. Regardless of how depressed and sad a person is, performing an action of sharing makes them a cause — as indeed does doing anything that fits this definition. If you are a teenager, for example, try this: without being asked, vacuum the carpets in your family home. If you are an adult, how about this: go to visit someone you know who is in hospital. The Perfect System doesn't even care if you are a walking zombie when you do it; just do it.

The more acts of giving you perform, the more experience you will have of being like a cause. The more you act like a cause, the easier it will be for you — any of you — to separate yourself from the Effect Line.

I remember my mother telling me a story about a woman who lived in a small town. Her best friend's husband had just passed away. She didn't know how to break her sadness over her friend's pain and loss, and she became depressed. But she had to do something. So, instinctively, during the mourning period, she went into her friend's hall closet, took out the late husband's shoes, and started to shine them. The widow was surprised when she saw her best friend on her hands and knees performing this menial task. She asked, "What are you doing?" The friend replied calmly, "I know that your husband didn't leave you much and that you will need money, so I thought I would shine his shoes for you so that they're ready for sale. I didn't know what else to do for you. I knew words would be meaningless to you right now, but I just needed to do something for you."

What she did may seem trite, even slightly ridiculous, but in this example, both women were fulfilled. Performing this action was the friend's only way to validate her relationship. She intuitively knew that only a physical action could reconnect her to the First Cause. You see, the more specific an action, the more potent the return.

We must never forget what it is we really want out of life: true, lasting fulfillment. I feel compelled to keep reiterating this point because it is the very foundation of our understanding of ourselves and our actions.

By taking any action, you are guaranteed to reap what you sow. It's also a hell of a lot more sensible than waiting for someone to knock on your door and give you what you want — but, most important, it works. I know the process can appear to be selfish in intent, yet in the big picture, selfless selfishness is, *in deed*, a true win-win proposition.

I know I am sounding like a broken record (or should I say a skipping CD), but judgments like "selfish" and "selfless," "good" or "bad," are words not used in the Perfect System. They're irrelevant because these rules and laws just are — they exist, they're real. "Good" and "bad" are also never used in the Perfect System because they are relative. The Perfect System by definition is absolute. For example, in our physical world, what is good for one person may be bad for another. If, for instance, I close a big deal in my business, it's very good for me — but it may also be very bad for my competitor, who didn't get the business. In love, what is good for the successful suitor is bad for the guy who lost out.

Which leads to another truth. Don't be too quick to judge a situation for its good or bad values. As reported in the press,

Jim Henson, who created the Muppets, sold his company to Disney for more than $100 million. Was it a good event or a bad event? I guess at the time it was a good event, but three or four days later it turned into a bad event because Jim Henson died of "walking pneumonia." Maybe it was the stress of the last-minute negotiations that aggravated his pneumonia and allowed it to take his life. Had he not been negotiating the deal, would he still be alive today? I had a friend who was in a car accident. While being x-rayed for possible injuries, the doctors found a malignant tumour. Had they not discovered the tumour at that time and operated, my friend would not be alive today. The cancer was removed and never returned. So, was his car accident a good or bad thing? Never be quick to judge and always look to the big picture. Life is funny that way!

At this point, there is one more principle I wish to remind you about. As I have stated before, the Perfect System is an equal-opportunity employer. If you stick your finger into an electrical socket and get a shock, is the electricity punishing you? No, of course not. It's just a law of physics and physiology in action: human finger + electrical socket = shock. The rules and laws of the Perfect System are similarly detached and inflexible, which is why knowing them is so empowering. Respecting this knowledge stops us from putting our fingers into the electrical sockets of life and having painful experiences. We just have to follow the rules, obey the laws.

Here are the steps for converting fear, sadness, and depression into control, contentment, and happiness:

1. Trust in the rules and laws of the Perfect System.
2. Separate yourself from your feelings.
3. If you can't separate yourself from your feelings, then perform a simple act of giving.

4. Perform more simple acts of giving.

5. Keep trying to separate yourself from your Effect Line.

6. When you can separate yourself from your Effect Line, be more specific in your choices of giving. This means giving the very thing that you most need to someone else.

If you need respect from co-workers, give respect to them first. If you want more compassion from loved ones, first be more compassionate with them. If you want friends to be more considerate, be more considerate to them. You will get exactly what you need. It's the law of cause and effect at play, once more, the law that is an intrinsic part of the Perfect System.

I need to discuss three more negative human traits before closing this chapter. Why is it that we feel hatred towards others? Why is it that we feel what we have is never enough? Now that you are into the groove of understanding the big picture, you probably know the answer. You know that the answer to any Why question must have something to do with the one thing that every human being needs and will do anything to get and keep — true, long-lasting fulfillment. By our nature, we feel some mix of hatred, greed, and envy whenever our nourishment is threatened. These emotions will always occur in any situation in which someone wants to take away or not feed into our sense of fulfillment. This is a critical building block of racism, sexism, and chauvinism — indeed, of any "ism." If someone is different from me, then I am unfamiliar with his or her method of giving or taking fulfillment. This fulfillment is so important to us that we instinctively go into a defensive posture whenever our fulfillment is at risk.

When we are with people we perceive to be different from us (different in speech, smell, look, culture, religion, etc.), we feel threatened because we don't know how they socially, culturally, physically, or verbally give and take fulfillment. For instance, misogynists hate women because they are irrationally afraid that women will take away their sense of fulfillment (sense of security, sense of control, etc.). To follow this understanding, our emotions of greed and envy come from our need to protect the fulfillment that we have or to obtain that which we think we lack.

Make a list of the people you feel threatened by. Consciously or subconsciously, you probably sense that they put at risk your need for fulfillment. However, this concern is irrational because we *own* our fulfillment. Fulfillment is inclusive and personal. It is directly related to our affinity with the first Cause / First Creator that was complete and total. Once we actualize this affinity, we too, by our innate hierarchical birthright, are complete and total. Our fulfillment cannot be reduced unless we consciously decide to give it to someone else. It cannot unknowingly be taken away from us.

19

When Bad Things Happen . . .

It may be the hardest of all to grasp: how do we explain what we consider wrongs done to good people by others, by fate, or by life's vagaries? If "bad" things happen, why do they happen? Here again we must consider "good" and "bad" as relative constructs. And we must remember that the seemingly opposed principles of order and chaos in fact exist alongside one another. However, this is an emotionally charged issue for me. It appears to be so unfair when we see a child who is sick or injured. What about the stories we hear about an innocent person being killed by a drunk driver in what seems a senseless accident? I wish I could avoid these questions and the issues they raise, but, like you, I need to know where these incidents fit within the Perfect System.

For a long time, I believed these random acts were just that — acts of randomness, anomalies in a world of generalities. In fact, proof that determinism and indeterminacy existed side by side in a tense and opposite harmony. But I would like to suggest to you an alternate viewpoint. Although the above explanation is solid in its cold, harsh intellectualism, there is, I believe, something else at play. The coexistence of determinism and free will clearly gives us an opportunity to control much that happens in our lives. We now can predict certain effects from a given action, and we can make a free-will decision about what effect it is that we want in return ("for every action there is an equal and opposite reaction"). However, for us to be in control of the complex formula of cause and effect and free will, one condition must be present: consciousness, a level of understanding of the big picture that allows us, at the most elemental level, to start choosing our destiny.

In the case of sick or injured children, they lack this elemental consciousness. We see it demonstrated all the time. Children run out into traffic chasing a ball. They touch a hot stove element or indiscriminately play with sharp objects. That's how they learn the big picture: by discovery, testing, and invention. This is why we must protect our children from the randomness of the universe until they reach the elemental level of consciousness of the big picture. They are truly innocent victims because they are not able to perceive the ultimate blend of cause and effect and randomness. They don't have the tools to predetermine an outcome in the way that we do now. As parents, we are guardians of their bodies and consciousness. This is why I believe we have absolute responsibility to teach them the concept of cause and effect at the youngest age possible. Give them the weaponry to create well-being in their lives.

The one caveat to this explanation is when a child is born with a deformity or terminal illness. I wish I had more wisdom around this issue, because events appear to be totally unbalanced. Cause and effect do not appear to be at play. This is randomness at its most inexplicable. My heart goes out to all who suffer this pain.

However, in the example of an innocent person being killed by a drunk driver, the two people are both participants in the classic play between determinism and indeterminacy. This apparently random type of accident is a warning and a reminder to us to always be alert and stay away from people who are unsharing and clearly self-interested, those who have desire only for themselves. These people are walking negative causes waiting to receive negative effects. When it is payback time — and payback time always comes ("for every action there is an equal and opposite reaction") — try not to be next to the person who has the payback coming. Plane crashes, auto accidents, and industrial injuries are all examples of this principle. To be crass, in the case of a car crash, your number may not be up, but the other driver's number may be. The one other consideration in what appears to be a random act against a good, innocent, decent person is that it may not be so random. This other possibility requires painful honesty. Decency, goodness, and innocence are surface descriptions. We project these general qualities onto others. However, we never know what is going on inside someone else's mind and heart.

What to do? Staying home and never leaving your bed is one solution. The problem with this course of action is that it is hard to get the true, long-lasting fulfillment we need by being recluses. We need other people to share with, to validate us, and to actualize our affinity with the First Cause. So the solution lies in constantly being on the alert to the principles of determinism and randomness (certainty and chaos) that are at work, side by side, at all times. Think all the time. Think about what you are doing and the consequences of your actions. Think about whom you are with. And just as important, sense the moment. The more you raise your consciousness, the more options and choices you will have.

~

I remember when I first visited Los Angeles. My brother, who lived there, warned me about the crazy drivers in La-La Land. While driving me to pick up a rental car, he said to me, "Before getting on the freeway, look to the left, look to the right, look in front of you, look behind you — do it all again, then enter the freeway." The next day, I read in the L.A. *Times* that a driver was killed on the freeway by a car crashing into him from above! A car went through a guardrail on an overpass and crashed into the car driving below. Bizarre, fluky, but tragically true.

Be careful out there! The more positive energy you can create coming back to you, the better chance you will have of controlling outcomes. Why is it that a person will miss by minutes catching a plane that later crashes? I can recall driving home late one night. There was a dense fog and I noticed as I was exiting the highway that the overhead lights on the off-ramp had blown. I couldn't see more than three feet in front of me. A premonition made me sharply swerve my car to the right. A split second later, I passed the image of a hitchhiker walking up the left side of the off-ramp. Had I not veered at that precise moment I would have hit him full force. One of us was protected by the positive energy we had accumulated — or perhaps it was a blend of both. We hear about such stories all the time. I believe that the more positive fulfillment you have coming back to you, the more protection you will have against the randomness that exists in this physical world.

To challenge our belief structures further: Why do we perceive death as the worst possible outcome? In the physical world, it is an inevitable reality. To those who lose close family and friends, no time is a good time for dying, whether someone is in his or her twenties or eighties. Mankind has always put a negative value on dying. But we know that we are limited by our five senses. There is much that exists in our world beyond their validation. Which leads to the question, why is death considered a "bad" thing? Remember that in the big picture there is no real bad or good. Death appears to be bad because we lose the physical presence of our loved ones. What about their energy? I would like to use the concept of light to illustrate this point. What is light? Science tells us it is both particle and wave form. Can we see light? Absolutely not! What we see is light being reflected or refracted. Without a surface to bounce off, light, to our sight, would not exist. In deep space, there is only darkness. Yet the sun is throwing off light rays all the time.

In much the same way, the value we put on physical death is distorted by what we think we know and see. No physical body, no person. This may sound metaphysical but it is not. It is the nature of the human experience to arbitrarily put values on events, to assign judgments. We have a compulsion to make sense of the stuff around us. But these are only opinions forged from our historical, physical, and experiential points of view. Take into consideration that these values are not sacrosanct.

Scientifically, we are just in the early stages of being able to understand and see the total big picture. For example, the new superstring theory postulates that there is a dimension that exists beyond that which we have previously understood — a world of vibration and subatomic resonance where all matter consists of tiny vibrating strings. Perhaps they exist in a place somewhere beyond the speed of light. How can we imagine post light speed when we live in a light speed reality? Heady stuff, yet this conceptual thinking is changing, and new thinking is changing the way we view reality. If the superstring theory is correct, then the whole concept of physicality being composed only of particles will also change. The earth, the universe, you, and I are just a series of oscillating strings vibrating in cosmic harmony, all players in the symphony of life.

Science has just touched the surface of the Perfect System. As we learn more and dig deeper into its inner workings, what other wonders will we discover? I have joined the concepts of death and superstring theory together to demonstrate that we should never be so self-assured and arrogant about what we think we know. The advice from the Perfect System is to be open-minded to all possibilities; to avoid jumping too quickly to determine the value of people, things, and events; and to always be mindful of the interplay of matter and energy within the system.

20

The Perfect Circle

In this last chapter, I need you now to see all the pieces of the puzzle together. Each jagged piece now joins to become the shape of a circle — the symbol of wholeness. The Perfect System is and will always be a single unity. The power of this unity is now yours.

With the learning that I hope you have received from this book, the Perfect System will become increasingly evident to you. Be conscious of your newfound knowledge. Take responsibility for your actions, and don't get frustrated when you forget to put into practice what you have learned. Think of a baby's frustration and patience when learning to crawl. You will be overcoming years of knee-jerk reactions. I never said it would be easy, but I do say it is possible. Real change takes time.

I find myself falling back into my own old ways when I am not on my toes, not fully alert. Being reactive is part of our nature and should be expected. Our job is to overcome this part of our nature and be proactive in all that we do. We have to learn to take control. We have to learn to be conscious at all times, to be awake. Most of the world sleeps. I will assure you of this: you will never be able to go back completely to your old ways again. If you have come this far in the book, then its truths have resonated inside you. Use the information. When you change yourself from an effect into a cause, wondrous things happen. Watch how your personal and business relationships change. Write down the changes so when you reach a slow period of growth, you can look back at all your new successes and recharge yourself with their power. Start right now!

Also remember that growth is not constant. There will be rapid periods of growth and slow periods, but don't despair — just know that a slow period precedes a faster one and that, although the speed of growth is not constant, you are always in a constant state of growth. It's the way of the Perfect System.

Remember: it's all about true, lasting fulfillment.

Epilogue

I speak on the subject of the Perfect System to public and business organizations around the country. One of the questions I am most often asked is what is my personal position on how physicality was created. Was it simply a random event or an act of purpose by a supernatural entity? In other words, do I believe in the existence of God?

My answer, which I base both on scientific theory and on personal intuition, is, emphatically, yes! The Creation had to be a purposeful action. Understand that my opinion is ultimately an assumption. But any answer to this question must be an assumption — on the yea or nay side. As well, my opinion is irrelevant to the universal truths expressed in this book. But here is how I came to my conclusion.

The First Creator/First Cause made the physical world *ex nihilo* (out of nothing). Science tells us that there suddenly appeared out of nothing an incredible source of energy in the form of a singularity. This singularity, this concentration of pure energy, this primeval fireball exploded outwards. This Big Bang expanded and eventually started to cool down and form matter. The atoms and molecules that were created from this cooling were the beginnings of our physical universe. They are the basic constituents of everything we see, touch, and sense in every way, ranging from rocks, trees, and animals to oceans, stars, and galaxies. The highest level of this "matter animation" is humankind. When you have something coming from nothing, you have, by my definition, an act of creation.

Being in a creative profession, I know that there are two imperatives to the creative process: first, there must be a desire or will to create, and second, given this will, creation must be manifested. In simpler terms, you can't paint a picture before wanting or desiring its creation. This is why I side with the idea that, at a point before the space-time continuum existed, something caused the process of Creation. Logic alone forces me to accept that Creation was not a random act, because even a random act needs a cause, and that cause needs another. Moreover, there is too much evidence of harmony and order in the manifested creation for me to conceive that the universe was a random creation. How could all this precision be the random effect of a random cause? Furthermore, there can be only one source of a cause: another cause. Yet — and here's the conundrum — by definition, the First Creator/First Cause has no precursor and thus must have had within itself the source of its causality. This is called will.

Those who can't relate to the logic here might more easily understand the other source of my certainty: it simply made sense to me, intuitively. I have always trusted my intuitive sense (right brain) over my rational sense (left brain). The left brain can be fooled a hell of a lot faster than the right brain because of the limitation of the five senses. The contemporary Jewish philosopher Abraham Joshua Heschel endorsed this notion when he wrote that "man apprehends more than he comprehends."

Intuitively, I saw that rules and laws governed the world I lived in. Trees didn't fly off into space. White clouds continued to float by in a blue sky. All around me, I saw a profound, complex process that was complete and true to itself. The world was, in effect, my other source of validation. What I believed to be true was also evident in its clockwork perfection, in its delicately balanced ecosystems, and in the sublime genius of the human body.

What came to epitomize this order for me, however, was the simple conversion cycle of evaporation, sublimation, and condensation of water. This orderly little process and the byproducts that stemmed from it made rain, made air, made electricity — and, ultimately, made the whole grand human experience possible. It was one of those personal, poignant observations that carried for me the profoundest message of all.

I also sensed that the Creator still existed in its creation. Its will continued to exist and was manifest in the laws and rules that kept the creation going in much the same way a painter's will and imagination never leave the canvas. It is as if an aspect or a part of the First Creator remained in the system.

The undeniable truth of this thought is that our world is made up of the previously mentioned opposites living in what should be an impossible harmony of determinism and indeterminacy. What could be a more perfect metaphor for the Creator and its creation? Simply put, the Creator had the will to create. In our terms, it had free choice of action. The Creator manifested this will in a physical creation that must, by definition, be material (held together by physical properties and laws). This is so beautifully obvious to me. It is the genius of the creation and the ultimate proof that causality and free will can exist side by side in our unpredictable, predictable world.

To reinforce my take on the Creation, I looked to other opinions. Below are a few selected ideas given by reputable members of the scientific community.

Here are the words and commentary of Alan Guth, a physicist at the Massachusetts Institute of Technology, as quoted from *Genesis and the Big Bang* by Gerald L. Schroeder (Bantam Books, New Sciences, 1990, used by permission).

[If you believe in the Big Bang theory] you believe that, once upon a time, all the potential of the cosmos — all the potential for a firmament of 40 billion galaxies at last count — was packed into a point smaller than a proton. You believe that within this incipient cosmos was neither hypercompressed matter nor superdense energy nor any tangible substance. It was a "false vacuum" through which coursed a weightless, empty quantum-mechanical probability framework called a "scalar field." You're probably not clear about what a scalar field is, but then neither are most PhDs.

Next, you believe that, when the big bang sounded, the universe expanded from a pinpoint to cosmological size in far less then one second — space itself hurtling outward in a torrent of pure physics, the bow wave of the new cosmos moving at trillions of times the speed of light.

Further, you believe that, as subatomic particles began to unbuckle from the inexplicable proto-reality, both matter and antimatter formed. Immediately, these commodities began to collide and annihilate themselves, vanishing as mysteriously as they came. The only reason our universe is here today is that the "Big Bang" was slightly asymmetrical, its yield favoring matter over antimatter by about one part per 100 million.

Because of this, when the stupendous cosmic commencement day ended, a residue of standard matter survived, and from it the galaxies formed. That is to say: You believe that a microscopic, transparent, empty point in primordial space-time contained not just one universe but enough potential for 100 million universes.

It's wise to take the "Big Bang" hypothesis seriously, since considerable evidence weighs in its favor. The galaxies are expanding away from one another as if they had once been in the same place, then hurled outward; the interstellar void is slightly warmer than absolute zero, suggesting the universe was once super-heated by something much stronger than the output of stars; the earliest nebulae appear to be composed of precisely the mix of elements that "Big Bang" calculations suggest.

Yet for sheer extravagant implausibility, nothing in theology or metaphysics can hold a candle to the Big Bang. Surely, if this description of the cosmic genesis came from the Bible or the Koran rather than MIT, it would be treated as a preposterous myth. Next, here is an excerpt from *In the Beginning* by Nathan Aviezer (Hoboken, N.J.: Ktav Publishing, 1990, used by permission). Aviezer is a professor of physics and chairman of the Physics Department at Bar-Illan University in Israel.

THE EARTH

Earth, Mars and Venus were all once covered with vast oceans and each had an atmosphere conducive to life. However, the development of Mars and Venus was such that on both of these planets all surface water disappeared in the course of time and their atmospheres became completely hostile to life. Why did the Earth escape these catastrophes? And are they properly termed catastrophes, because man cannot survive without water?

The answer is that Earth escaped these catastrophes by sheer accident! The Earth just happened to be sufficiently distant from the Sun that the runaway greenhouse effect did not occur and therefore all our surface water neither evaporated nor decomposed. Moreover, the Earth just happened to be sufficiently near the Sun that it remained warm enough to prevent all the oceans from freezing permanently into ice caps. Therefore, the Earth, alone among the planets of the solar system, is capable of supporting human life. It is quite remarkable that the Earth is precisely the required distance from the Sun to support human life.

Recent studies of the carbonate-silicate geo-chemical cycle have made it increasingly clear that the planetary atmosphere is controlled by a very delicate balance, involving the subtle interplay of many factors, which determines whether or not life can exist. This balance is so delicate that if the Earth were only a few percent closer to the Sun, surface temperatures would be far higher than the boiling point of water, precluding all possibility of life. Similarly, if the Earth were only a few percent farther from the Sun, the concentration of carbon dioxide in the atmosphere would be so high the atmosphere would not be breathable by human beings. Thus, the orbit of the Earth just happened to be at a distance from the Sun that is in a very narrow habitable zone within which liquid water could condense.

These phenomena have attracted considerable scientific interest and have been named the "anthropic principle."

THE MOON

The weather we experience today is directly related to the influence of the Moon on the Earth. The existence of the Moon is the result of a series of "accidental occurrences." It was recently shown by Professor Cameron of Harvard University that the Moon resulted from "the impact on the earth of a planetary body a little larger than Mars." Our Moon is thus unique, having been formed by a process quite different from that responsible for the formation of the other moons of the solar system. He and his colleagues have demonstrated that the Moon would not have resulted from a collision between planetary bodies unless certain stringent conditions were met. Our Moon was formed from a planetary collision because the colliding body just happened to have the required mass, just happened to have the required relative velocity and angle of collision and just happened to have the required composition for its core and mantle. If these constraints on the motion and composition of the colliding body had not been satisfied, then the collision would have been shattering and no Moon would have formed.

THE SUN

The very existence of living organisms on this planet is due to another, "accidental occurrence." Life on Earth depends on the Sun, whose heat and light are the primary source of all terrestrial energy. Without the Sun there would not even be an Earth, much less a planet capable of supporting life.

In order for the thermonuclear reaction that takes place on the Sun [to happen], two conditions must be met. First, a proton must be able to combine with a neutron to form a deuteron (fuel must be present). Secondly, a proton must be unable to combine with another proton (explosive material must be absent). The possibility of proton-neutron combination and the possibility proton-proton combination both depend on the strength of the nuclear force. If the nuclear force was only a few percent weaker or a few percent stronger, the Sun would cease to shine. It is extraordinary that the nuclear force just happens to lie in the narrow range of the few percentage points required for thermonuclear reaction.

The numerous "accidents of nature" that seem to have happened for the existence and well-being of humankind have prompted many scientists to comment on the phenomenon. For example, Professor Freeman J. Dyson of the Institute for Advanced Studies in Princeton has stated this perception: "As we look out into the universe and identify the many accidents of physics and astronomy that have worked together to our benefit, it almost seems as if the universe must in some sense have known that we were coming."

And, finally, scientists are making observations that are stunning the world. In 1982 a remarkable event took place. At the University of Paris a research team led by physicist Alain Aspect performed what may turn out to be one of the most important experiments of the twentieth century. You did not hear about it on the evening news. In fact, unless you are in the habit of reading scientific journals, you probably have never even heard Aspect's name, though there are some who believe his discovery may change the face of science.

Aspect and his team discovered that under certain circumstances subatomic particles such as electrons are able to instantaneously communicate with each other regardless of the distance separating them. It doesn't matter whether they are ten feet or ten billion miles apart. When the rotation of one electron was changed the other separated electron changed its rotation at exactly the same time.

It was as if somehow each particle always knew what the other was doing.

I have said it before and I will say it again. Whether you believe in a random or purposeful creation of the universe, it is irrelevant to the knowledge expressed in this book. I hesitated to write this epilogue for fear of diminishing that value. No opinion in this matter carries more weight than another. My decision was ultimately based on my need to be totally open and exposed to you. And doing so allows for the completion of my story.

Thank you for going through this journey of discovery with me. To make it as interactive as possible, you can reach me at www.theperfectsystem.com; I will try to answer all inquiries, to the best of my abilities.

~

To close, I must confess that writing this book has been a difficult challenge for me. I am a proud and private person. So, having to expose my stupidity and insensitivity in my personal life and then my fall from grace in my business life has been not cathartic but heart-wrenching. But I knew that to be totally sharing, I had to come clean — warts and all. I believe that the information contained in this book is more potent and relevant because it was framed by my life experience.

Do not be misled by the seeming simplicity of the Perfect System. It is not some haphazard collection of common-sense homilies. It is a system that is integrated and flawless. Move one thing and another thing moves in harmony someplace else. It is joined and we are all joined in it. The Perfect System is not about philosophy or theology. The question is not, "If a tree falls in a forest and there is no one there, does it make a sound?" The question is, "I am in the forest and a tree is about to fall on me. What do I do?" The Perfect System gives us the knowledge and subsequent ability to get out of harm's way.

We never want to feel empty. I can't repeat this notion enough. What motivates us is our need for long-lasting fulfillment. We all need to feel loved, safe, secure, and connected to our origins.

And to complete the thought, we are responsible for achieving this fulfillment. Our lack of fulfillment is never someone else's fault or responsibility.

I would now like to thank all the readers who had the patience and resolve to read to the end of this book. I was given a wondrous gift, and I have tried to share it with you. We are now joined in this experience for all time. May you all be able to change your lives for the better using the rules and laws of the Perfect System.

Close your eyes and imagine everything you could possibly want and need in your life. Now multiply it by a thousand times. This is what I wish for you, that all your desires and dreams come true, far beyond your imagination.